Vicki Gordy's book, A Heart for God: Lovin[*fresh air! Unlike so many other books focusi* *sincerity and concern rather than simply offeriing an...* *sure, Gordy offers her readers plenty of answers and a number of good reasons for believing in and trusting Jesus as Lord, but* A Heart for God *also offers the reader a glance into the author's heart—a heart that loves God and her neighbors. In short, this book was a labor of love, and it shows. Fortunately, truth and love are not mutually exclusive, and* A Heart for God *is thus an example of how to speak—or write—the truth in love (Ephesians 4:15). As a result,* **I predict that readers will come away with a sense that the Gospel is worth serious consideration,** *and a healthy respect for the author of this wonderful book.*

— **Bob Stewart**
Professor of Philosophy and Theology
Director of the Apologetics Program
New Orleans Baptist Theological Seminary

A Heart for God *is a wonderful book for everyone whether you're curious about Christianity's truth claims and teachings or you're a Christian who wants to grow in your understanding of what you believe and why. Vicki's sincere desire to demonstrate why Christ is trustworthy is evident on every page. She combines her own story about why she became a Christian with rigorous scholarship and plausible answers to questions commonly asked about Christianity. Her writing is accessible to everyone from those familiar with the apologetics content in the book or just encountering it for the first time.* **A Heart for God** *includes some of the best reasons to believe that Christianity is true, but Vicki doesn't just speak to the mind. She engages the mind and heart, inviting readers to accept God's invitation to reconciliation with Him through Christ.*

— **Lanie Anderson**
MDiv in Christian Apologetics
lanieanderson.com

Instead of sidestepping the questions of creation and the existence of God, this book embraces these questions and analytically considers the options in an easy-to-understand format that can be appreciated by everyone. I believe that this approach serves well to invite the person with rational doubts in finding comfort through a rational understanding of the possibilities. It's a compelling read that allows the reader to make a better decision as to what is truly believable. **This analytical approach offered a refreshing and unpressured read and opened my mind and heart with a perspective and understanding for which I am most grateful.**

— **Dr. Joseph Lacoste, Jr**.
Founder and CEO
Louisiana Dental Center

As I began to read Vicki's book, I felt she was speaking to me and not at me. *I read* A Heart for God *over a weekend and again the next week. This book of testimony and apologetics fits smoothly between the introductory thoughts in* More Than a Carpenter *and the complexity of* Evidence that Demands a Verdict. **Vicki shows great skill, patience, and depth of research in writing this book. I have ordered a large supply to share with my friends and disciples.**

— **Barry Haindel**
Director
Life Resources

A HEART FOR GOD

A HEART FOR GOD

Loving God with Your Whole Heart

VICKI LYNN GORDY

Printed in the United States of America by BookBaby Publishing

Cover design: Lisa Vento

www.heartforgod.org

I dedicate this book to my family, to future family members, and to all who read it. May God bless you as you seek to know him and to love him with your whole heart.

INDEX

Acknowledgements

I'm grateful to Dr. Robert M. Bowman, Jr., Dr. Daniel B. Wallace and his interns at the Center for the Study of New Testament Manuscripts (Zachary Skarka, Ben Min, and Leigh Ann Hyde), Dr. Raymond Stewart, Dr. David Calhoun, Pastor John Frady, Lanie Anderson, and Marilyn Stewart, who each reviewed portions of the manuscript (or the manuscript in its entirety) and offered helpful comments. Their feedback greatly strengthened this work. Still, I am responsible for the final product and the opinions expressed herein.

Others who helped in various ways or encouraged me in this process include Eric and Amy Smith, Jim and Tammy Gordy, Joey and Gwen Lacoste, Dr. Robert Stewart, Sancy Eshenour, Jodie Tjon, Joe Fontenot and Vickie Dauphin Dewey.

I appreciate you all, and I am very thankful for your help in making my vision for A Heart for God a reality.

Preface

Late one July afternoon in 2014—a week to the day before my 60th birthday—my phone rang. The words I heard would totally interrupt my life.

At this point, the book I wanted to write someday was a two-inch thick folder with loose pages of random thoughts, Bible verses, and quotations I had been compiling for a couple of years. I wanted to put together the most important messages I could share: what I came to learn during my life's journey about God, the Bible, and Jesus and why my decision to follow Jesus was the best decision I ever made. I would also share how God's amazing plan for us—this life-giving and life-transforming treasure that I discovered many years ago—is available to anyone who sincerely wants it. There is nothing more valuable I could pass on to those I love and to future generations.

Originally, I envisioned writing this book for my family, but later my vision expanded beyond family. I thought about this book frequently and considered it a hobby I would work on leisurely over the next ten years. It was one of the top items on my list of goals I hoped to complete before I turned 70.

But time stood still when I received that phone call. I learned that my biopsy results were positive for breast cancer. I was informed the following day the specific type of breast cancer was "triple negative" (TNBC), which soon after I discovered has been described as the fastest growing breast cancer that is also hardest to treat and most likely to recur.

As one might imagine, that news was quite sobering. A lot of soul-searching follows this type of diagnosis.

Anyone in this situation can't help but wonder, "What if my time on this earth is short?" "Is there any unfinished business in my life?" I was at peace for the most part. However, there were two areas in which I desired more time.

At that time, my daughter Amy (my only child) was 28. I hoped I would live long enough to see more of her life unfold and to be here for her. I eventually came to a place of acceptance, though, that regardless of my outcome, she would be okay. I realized no time would ever feel like the *right time* to leave her, even if I were a hundred years old. I trusted that God would be with her, as would so many people who love and care about her.

Considering how fast-growing this cancer is, I also felt sad that I might not realistically be able to complete the book I so wanted to write if this was the beginning of the end of my life.

But I spent very little time focusing on the "what if" question. During most of my journey with cancer, I felt a very strong sense of peace. I came to accept that whatever the outcome of this illness would be, I could trust that God knows best how my life should play out to accomplish his purposes for me, and that gave me comfort.

The next nine months were a whirlwind of activity. In addition to the medical treatment I had locally in the New Orleans area, I made numerous six-hour commutes from my home to M. D. Anderson Cancer Center in Houston. On April 14, 2015, I officially completed my treatment. Gratefully, at the end of it all, I received a good prognosis.

I am so thankful to God that I've been cancer-free for several years now. During this time, I've enjoyed many very special moments with family and friends, including two of the most wonderful days of my life: the marriage of my daughter and son-in-law and the birth of my granddaughter.

I am also full of gratitude to God for the time he has given me to complete this book. Writing it has been a wonderful and fulfilling experience I will always treasure. Throughout the process, I have been strengthened, convicted, humbled, inspired, motivated, and stretched. My hope and prayer is that God blesses *you* through this book in some way, too.

I am so happy to be able to share my journey with you! So here it is, from my heart to yours, *A Heart for God…*

Introduction

"People look at the outward appearance, but the LORD looks at the heart."
(I Samuel 16:7)
"So we fix our eyes not on what is seen, but on what is unseen, since what is seen is temporary, but what is unseen is eternal." (2 Corinthians 4:18)

There is so much more to you than the reflection you see in the mirror.

Although your body is part of your personhood and God's Word is clear that your body has great value, the most important part of you is unseen—that is, your inner self. The Bible often refers to your inner self as your "heart." This word is mentioned over 700 times in the Bible, but very few times is it referring to the physical heart. Author James W. Sire says "In short, and in biblical terms, the heart is 'the central defining element of the human person.'"[1]

Your heart is invisible to the human eye, yet others get to know your heart by what you reveal through your life—what you say and do and, sometimes, by what you don't say and don't do. "As water reflects the face, so one's life reflects the heart" (Proverbs 27:19).

While people see only what you reveal through outward expressions of your life, God sees beyond. He sees your heart. Your heart matters to him—more than you might know.

It has been said that the One who knows you the best loves you the most. He knows you better than anyone else, and for that matter, he knows you better than you know yourself. He loves you beyond human comprehension.

His desire is that you would love him back… with your whole heart.

REASONS TO BELIEVE

REASONS TO BELIEVE

"But in your hearts honor Christ the Lord as holy, always being prepared to make a defense to anyone who asks you for a reason for the hope that is in you." (I Peter 3:15 ESV)

Not everyone reading this book believes the Bible is reliable, Jesus is who he claimed to be, or that God exists. Obviously, a person can't love God if they don't even think he exists. As author and Christian apologist Josh McDowell said, "A heart cannot rejoice in what the mind rejects."[1] I know this from personal experience…

A JOURNEY TO BELIEF

When I was young, my opportunities to learn about God were limited. We attended church for a brief time when I was about nine years old and then again around age eleven. I also attended church for several years during high school with someone I dated. But the church experiences I had growing up didn't have an immediate impact on my life.

I began college at age 17. It felt strange to be in this new *adult* environment. It was different, exciting and somewhat intimidating. At first, I remember being naively in awe of the professors. My history class was huge—it was held in an auditorium. I don't remember the professor's name, but what he taught me affected my life for several years to come.

This professor stated it is not historically accurate to believe Jesus existed. He claimed Jesus was just a myth. At the time, I assumed he knew what he was talking about. After all, he was the *history* professor. I thought he certainly wouldn't make such comments unless he had facts to back up what he was saying.

After that semester, I transferred to an out-of-town college and my mother gave me a Bible when I left home. I occasionally picked it up and skimmed through it, but deep down I thought if I were intellectually honest with myself (based on what my history professor taught me), I would conclude that Jesus was probably just a myth and God must be a myth, too.

I only attended college for three semesters. My college experience was short, but it was long enough for me to learn a few life lessons, one being that professors are certainly not all-knowing. The history professor's comments were now in question. But at this point in my life, any desire to revisit the belief-in-God issue was put on hold due to the many distractions available to young adults like me.

Several years later at age 21, I began to form my own identity and beliefs. Like a lot of young adults, I was no longer willing to accept thoughts and opinions just because I had been taught them. I also had those nagging questions about life, such as: "Where did I come from?" "Why am I here?" And, "Where am I going?" I felt increasingly compelled to reconsider whether God is real or a myth, and to stop pushing this aside every time it came to mind. I wanted to know the truth. If I reached the conclusion that God is not real, I could put it all to rest. If I came to believe he is real, that would be significant, and I would want to acknowledge that belief in my life. But I had to sincerely believe he is real. I didn't want to just go through the motions.

One quiet fall evening after I arrived home from work, I was bored and looking for something to do. I went to my bookshelf, picked up *Peace with God* by Billy Graham and began reading it. (The book caught my eye several months earlier and I bought it with the intention of reading it at some point in the future.) After reading through a few thought-provoking chapters, I remember pausing to reflect on what was written. I walked over to the window of my second-floor apartment and looked out at a stunningly beautiful sunset. I remember gazing in awe of the beauty of creation. At that moment, everything began to unfold.

"Where did I come from?" Obviously, man is not capable of creating the sky, the sun and the trees I viewed outside my window. If man did not create this universe, then I thought it logically follows that a form of being *lower* than man couldn't have created it. When I considered the intricacies, the majesty, and the order of the universe, it seemed unreasonable to me that no intelligent force was behind it all. If neither man nor a form of being lower than man is capable of creation, then, by process of elimination, I concluded that a form of being greater than man must have created it all. Then I thought, "Okay. This is who we know as God."

"Why am I here?" If God created us, I was sure he had purposes in mind for doing so. Purposes known to him. Purposes for us to discover. I remembered learning through my earlier church experiences that the Bible is one of the ways God speaks to us, and Graham's chapters I had just read confirmed this teaching. I thought the Bible could help me learn more about God and answer some of my questions.

"Where am I going?" Although I knew almost nothing about the Bible, I remembered some of the basic messages it taught—that God loves us so much he came to earth in the human form of Jesus to help us know him better, and that his death on the cross provided an opportunity for us to enter into a relationship with him, offering us a clean slate from all of our sins and a new way to think and live. I also knew the Bible teaches that although these earthly bodies of ours won't last forever, we will live on with or without God, and he has given us a free will to choose which path we will take.

Even though Jesus' death on the cross as payment for our sins and eternity were not easy concepts for me to understand, I considered that, in my humanness, there are mysteries and dimensions of reality I simply was not designed with the capacity to comprehend, at least while on this earth.

It all began to make sense to me, and I couldn't just ignore the significance of what now seemed logical, reasonable, and obvious.

It was time. Time for a decision. Time for a change. Time for me to express to God what was on my heart: that I had lived the first 21 years of my life without really knowing him. That I was sorry for my sins, and I needed and wanted his forgiveness. That I wanted to know him and learn why he created me and how he wanted me to live. And that I needed him to guide me. On the evening of October 16, 1975, this was my prayer.

So it was, over forty years ago, when my college professor tried to persuade us to disbelieve the claims of Christianity. That was in the context of a culture in which almost everyone accepted God's existence and identified as a Christian. Today the voices denying his existence and challenging Christianity are louder and greater in number, especially in the college setting. Unfortunately, people too often accept this information (like I did at first) with little to no scrutiny.

If you have heard or read claims that cause you to doubt God's existence, the Bible's reliability, or that Jesus' claims are true, I invite you to explore further. Discover why others who have heard this same information have not been convinced by it. Why are they persuaded that these claims are either untrue or irrelevant? What additional information do they have? How did they reach different conclusions?

At this point, you might be thinking, "Doesn't that go both ways? I've heard claims about God and Christianity throughout my life. How do I know they are true?" I'm glad you asked! Yes, it does go both ways. No one needs to believe in God, the Bible, and Jesus without good reason. This is where Christian apologetics comes in.

What exactly is Christian "apologetics?" First let me clarify a common point of confusion about this word. Although the spelling of this word is almost identical to the term "apologetic," the meaning of "apologetics" has nothing to do with an apology. The term "apologetics" comes from the Greek word "apologia" and means "defense." This word is defined as "reasoned arguments of writing in justification of something, typically a theory or religious doctrine."[2]

Christian apologetics explains why it is reasonable to believe in God, Jesus and the Bible through the academic disciplines of history, archaeology, philosophy, science, physics and math.

As a result of what I experienced with my professor, I have always had an interest in defenses for the Christian faith. The first apologetics-type book I read was *More Than a Carpenter* by Josh McDowell. Some years later I discovered C. S. Lewis. Many more Christian apologists are on the scene today.

Additionally, in recent years I have had the pleasure of serving as a volunteer for apologetics events featuring top apologists from around the nation and other parts of the world. I've also seen many dialogues between Christian apologists and highly renowned skeptics of Christianity. Between these dialogues and other resources, I haven't just heard one side of the issues. I've heard both sides extensively and doing so has only served to strengthen my belief in, and passion for, the God of the Bible.

For those interested in discovering why so many believe in the claims of Christianity, more resources are available today than ever before. The increased challenges to Christian beliefs in the last few decades have created the need for better articulation of why we believe what we believe and easier access to this information. As a result, Christian apologetics has exploded in recent years, providing an abundance of books, videos, and websites. The discussion of apologetics has increased at many churches from their pulpits to their Bible studies. Ministries and clubs specifically focused on apologetics are popping up as well. In recent years, even a few movies with an apologetics message like *The Case for Christ* have been released. There are also apologetics events such as seminars and conferences. The bottom line? There are resources galore for those interested in exploring evidence for the claims of the Christian faith.

The purpose of apologetics is not just to gain head knowledge about God, Jesus, and the Bible. Think of apologetics not as an end in itself but as a means to several ends—for believers and non-believers.

If you're already a believer, apologetics can stretch and deepen your own faith. It can also help you to help others. Being able to better defend the claims of Christianity is useful when people you encounter have questions and doubts. In cases where you are not able to answer a specific question posed to you, you'll at least be more familiar with helpful resources you can recommend. Even if you don't personally feel you need more evidence for the claims of Christianity because you're already convinced of their truthfulness, consider becoming "prepared to make a defense"[3] of what you believe for the benefit of others.

If you're not a believer but open to exploring Christianity, apologetics resources can be very helpful. When you think about it, what do you have to lose? At the end of your research, if you think the information is unconvincing, you will have at least expanded your horizon. You will be more well-read about Christianity, the religion of an estimated 2.2 billion people. At a minimum, you will have gained some knowledge about the world's largest religion. In your study of apologetics you also might discover some new information worth considering. Note these words of C.S. Lewis: "Christianity is a statement which, if false, is of no importance, and, if true, of infinite importance. The one thing it cannot be is moderately important."[4] If the claims of Christianity are not true, then it has no bearing on your life now or after you die. But, *if* these claims are true, this is not something that is just somewhat important—it is of infinite importance to you and to us all.

In the upcoming chapters, I will share some reasons why I am a follower of Jesus. Based on what I've learned through the years, I'm convinced that God is real, the Bible is reliable, and Jesus is who he claimed to be. I will just scratch the surface of apologetics here. Should you desire to dig deeper into apologetics, excellent resources are available by biblical scholars who cover in much more depth the topics I introduce. A list of recommended resources is included on my website: heartforgod.org.

Before we delve into reasons for believing in God, the Bible and Jesus, let's first step back and look at a broader topic, the appropriate basis for *all* belief: truth.

PURSUING TRUTH

"To turn away from the great questions and dilemmas of life is a tragedy, for the quest for meaning and truth makes life worth living." [1] (Charles Colson)

The more we live in harmony with truth, the better. Living in harmony with truth begins by knowing the truth.

We have a natural curiosity about the world in which we live. We want to understand what is true about it and what is true about us. Through the ages, we have especially wanted to know the truth about life's most compelling questions: "What is the origin of the universe and man?" "Who are we?" "What is the meaning and purpose of our life?" "How can we live out our purpose?" And "What happens to us when we die?"

Our answers to these questions form the very core of our belief system, and the term used to describe our core beliefs is "worldview." We all have a worldview, whether or not we can explain what it is.

Our worldview not only represents our beliefs about life's deepest questions. We operate from our worldview. It is the lens through which we interpret the world around us, influencing what we think about ourselves and others, how we perceive our life experiences, and how we view what happens in the world.

Since our worldview impacts every aspect of our life, evaluating our core beliefs that make up our worldview is important. Our beliefs shouldn't be based on false assumptions, misinformation, emotions, or what we hope to be true. We should earnestly seek the truth so we will have greater confidence that what we believe is, in fact, true.

TRUTH DEFINED

Many misperceptions about truth exist today. When seeking truth about life's biggest questions, or any other topic, it is necessary to know some facts about truth—what it is and what it is not.

Truth is reality.

Truth is simply a representation of what is real. Truth is not based on personal opinions and feelings (i.e., it is not *subjective*). Truth is *objective*, based on facts and reality.

Some truths are visible, and some are invisible.

Reality is not determined only by what we are capable of seeing.

Even scientists believe in things they can't see or touch. There was a time when this was not true, but that changed several hundred years ago with the discovery of such things as gravity, magnetic fields, and momentum. All of these things exist, but none of them can be seen through a microscope. They are invisible.

It is a fact that material (visible) realities exist and immaterial (invisible) realities exist.

Truth is truth regardless of how we respond to it.

If something is true, it is true whether or not we know it, believe it, understand it, or like it.

- I may not *know* that mixing baking soda and vinegar will cause a chemical reaction, but if I mix baking soda and vinegar the reaction will still take place.

- Someone can *believe* something false, but their belief that it's true doesn't make it true.

- I may not *understand* how lightning strikes the earth, but lightning striking the earth is a reality whether or not I understand it.

- We don't *like* that we and our loved ones will die one day, but death is a fact regardless of how we feel about it.

So, truth is not contingent on us—on what we know, believe, understand, or like. Truth exists apart from us, independent of us.

People can have contrary beliefs, but there are no contrary truths.

This point is known in classic logic as the "law of non-contradiction" (and sometimes called the "law of contradiction"). Something cannot be true and false at the same time. My car is not both a Honda and not a Honda. It is not both true and false that I was in Louisiana when I wrote this paragraph.

The law of non-contradiction applies to all truths, including religious truths. This means that not all religious claims can be true. Since religions sometimes make opposite claims about what is true, some claims are true, and some are false.

If I say I believe God exists and someone else says, "That is your truth, but my truth is that God does not exist," it is true that we have different opinions or beliefs, but the statements we made are not both true. One statement is true. The other statement is false. Regardless of what we believe, God either exists or God does not exist. If we have a wrong opinion about God's existence, our opinion does not change what is true.

It is not true for me that Jesus is God in human form and true for someone else that Jesus is not God in human form. One statement is true. The other is false. Either Jesus is God in human form, or he is not. This truth is independent of what we believe.

A truth claim that is misrepresented or misapplied does not determine the validity of the claim.

If my doctor prescribed medicine for me to take three times a day, could I rightfully go back to the doctor and complain that the medicine didn't help if either I didn't take it at all or only took it once a day? If I said, "This medicine doesn't work," would that be a true statement? There is a truth about whether or not that medicine would have been effective for me, but the truth of its effectiveness cannot be determined if I do not take it as it was designed to be taken.

When someone does not properly represent, or apply, a philosophy or theory, that philosophy or theory cannot rightfully be judged as false if it has been misrepresented or misapplied. Likewise, the truth about a religion cannot be rightfully assessed by the misrepresentation or misapplication of it.

We cannot create truth, but we can discover truth.

We did not create this universe, so we did not decide what is true about it (its purpose, what it contains, what it looks like, and how it operates).

No human mind decided what the laws of physics would be, or that there would be stars in the sky, or that planets would revolve around the sun. We didn't determine that here on our planet we would have oceans with fish, mountains, trees, insects, animals, and mankind.

We had no part in deciding truths about humanity—that we would have two eyes, or a liquid we call blood flowing through our veins. We did not decide that our temperature would be approximately 98.6 degrees Fahrenheit, or that we would require hours of sleep each night. We made none of these decisions.

We had no say in the existence and operation of our invisible (immaterial) qualities like our consciousness and ability to think, dream, and experience emotions.

We also did not decide the moral code of this life—what is in our best interest (and what is not) for us to thrive physically, emotionally, relationally, and spiritually. We had no say in any of this because we did not create any of this.

Of course, there are things we can *create*. We can create art and music and books and meals and woodwork and myriads of other things, but we cannot create anything that is material or immaterial from nothing. When we create something material, we begin with some form of existing matter that we did not create. When we create

28

something immaterial, like music, we do so with the imagination of a mind that we also had no part in creating.

Although we cannot create truth, we have the ability to discover many truths. The Greek word for truth is *aletheia*. Some words used to define *aletheia* are "disclosure," "unclosedness," and "unconcealdness" — indicating that truth already exists.[2] Truth is hidden, and we simply *disclose* truth or discover it. We have the innate desire to know things (curiosity). We have internal clues about what is true (instincts). We have senses to assess truth and the ability to explore options, think, comprehend, reason, and reach logical conclusions.

We cannot know all truth, but we can know what we need to know.

Knowing all truth would mean we know everything there is to know—about everyone who has ever lived and about everything else in the universe. No person can know all truth.

It is easy for us human beings to have an inflated opinion of our capabilities. With all of our accomplishments and the knowledge we've acquired, it's easy to see mankind as the pinnacle of this universe. But let's look at some facts.

First, we are small. No... I mean *really, really* small. For starters, Earth is part of a galaxy. In the context of our galaxy Earth is a very tiny dot. Now, let's back up and consider that our galaxy is just one of over two trillion galaxies in our universe! That's right. In 2016, NASA estimated there are at least two trillion galaxies.[3] So we start off with this very tiny dot called Earth in our galaxy in the midst of two trillion other galaxies in the universe. Then living on this tiny dot are billions of us. Now, just imagine how small you/we are in relation to the universe! A very sobering thought. (If this thought makes you feel quite invisible and insignificant, hold on. More on this is coming in a later chapter. For now, let the fact sink in about how small we are.)

Not only are we really small, but we also have many limitations. We watch birds soaring through the sky, but we were not designed with the ability to fly. Dogs have a sense of smell and hearing that far exceeds ours. Cats can jump five to six times their length from a standing position. We can't do that. Birds, dogs and cats can do things we cannot do because of our limitations. Likewise, although the human brain and mind have amazing capabilities, we do not have the ability to know all there is to know. In the words of Sir Isaac Newton who was considered by some to be the foremost physicist of all time, "What we know is a drop. What we don't know is an ocean." [4]

Because our earthly capacity for knowledge is limited, there will always be some unanswered questions in our worldview, as there are in every worldview. No matter how carefully thought out and researched a worldview is, it will include some mysteries and questions that cannot be answered. We are simply not capable of comprehending or knowing some dimensions of reality in our human state.

Although we may not know all we would like to know, we can know what we need to know. We have the ability and opportunity to acquire the knowledge we need for our purposes on Earth.

TRUTH MISIDENTIFIED

> *"See to it that no one takes you captive through hollow and deceptive philosophy."* (Colossians 2:8)

There are various flawed ideologies about truth accepted in our world today. We will hone in on three of the most prevalent ones. The first ideology denies the *existence* of absolute truth. It is known as "relativism." The second rejects the *relevance* of truth. It's called "post-truth." The third, "scientism," teaches that *science alone* is the means to determine all truth. Here is a look at the problems with these philosophies.

Relativism

Relativism claims there are no absolute truths—no such thing as something being universally true or false, right or wrong, good or evil. We create our own reality and decide our own truths. In other words, truth exists only *within* us. Relativism also claims that everyone's views of what is true, false, right, wrong, good and evil are equally valid.

Although some fully embrace a relativistic way of thinking, others think in relative terms only regarding morality. This is known as "moral relativism," and it is the most widely accepted form of relativism. Those who think this way believe some things are true and false, but that everything related to morality is subjective—that there is no universal standard of right or wrong, good or evil.

Regardless of how relativism is applied, there are serious holes in this theory. Here are some:

First, the overarching declaration relativism makes is that there are no absolute truths. But this claim is a contradiction of itself (known as a "self-defeating statement"). By its own definition relativism can't even claim to be true since it argues that *nothing* is absolutely true. If nothing is absolutely true, this would include the theory of relativism. Additionally, claiming there are *no* absolute truths is another self-defeating statement because a claim with no exceptions is itself an absolute claim.

Relativism is also contradictory. It professes that *everyone's* version of truth is equal. However, if someone believes that something can be absolutely true or false, right or wrong, good or evil, according to relativism, such a belief would be false. So, relativism once again contradicts its own claim.

Here are some examples of how relativism would play out in the following circumstances.

- If I say, "I don't care what the pictures from outer space show, I believe the earth is flat," that would be my truth. No one can question my truth that the earth is flat. But we know this is a distortion of reality.

- If a man says it is perfectly acceptable to beat his wife when she does something he doesn't like, we would have no basis for challenging this man's thinking. If we object to his behavior, he could say, "You have your truth and I have mine." But we know this behavior is wrong.

- Since relativism espouses that everyone's viewpoints are equally true, that means there would be no difference in the moral acceptability of Mother Teresa's views about how to treat people versus Hitler's views about how to treat people. We would have no basis for saying the way Mother Teresa treated people is good and the way Hitler treated people is evil. But we know what Hitler did is evil, and we know what Mother Teresa did is good.

Regardless of one's philosophy of truth, these are a few examples showing that at our core we all know some things are absolutely true or false, right or wrong, good or evil, even if we claim that absolute truths do not exist. If someone believes the earth is flat, how many who claim that truth is relative would honestly accept this belief as equal to their own belief that the earth is spherical? How many would champion the rights of a man who believes there is nothing wrong with beating his wife? How many would defend the idea that Hitler had a right to treat people as he did simply because he believed he was doing the right thing?

Consistent application of relativism in everyday circumstances is also unrealistic. There are many instances in which people (regardless of their truth philosophy) expect or even demand absolute truth. We want the absolute truth from our family and friends, our bank, our doctor, our justice system, our government, and in many other life scenarios.

Despite the flaws of relativism, people throughout societies across the globe are embracing this ideology with open arms. While some may claim to be "relativists," I would venture to say most do not have a clue that the way they think is called "relativism," or understand its flaws. In most cases, they are just going with the flow of our culture, unknowingly falling "captive" (as the Bible calls it) to this "deceptive philosophy."

Post-truth

With a post-truth mindset, beliefs are driven by emotions, not facts.

"Post-truth" is defined as "relating to or denoting circumstances in which objective facts are less influential in shaping public opinion than appeals to emotion and personal belief." [5] In other words, how we feel about something, and what we believe (even if there is no factual basis for what we believe) matters more to us than objective facts.

The term post-truth was Oxford Dictionary's 2016 word of the year.[6] Oxford also noted that although the term post-truth meant something slightly different in the first known use of the word in 1992, for approximately the decade prior to 2016 its implied meaning is that truth itself has become irrelevant. If there is a conflict between the facts and what we *want* to believe based on our feelings, the facts are simply ignored or downplayed.

Post-truth is very much akin to relativism. Whereas relativism denies the existence of absolute truth, post-truth might as well deny its existence because it has rendered facts, reality, and truth as virtually irrelevant and unnecessary in forming one's beliefs. With this post-truth way of thinking, judgments are neither well thought out, nor based on logic and reasoning. Too often there is little to no effort to seek facts, to analyze, and to evaluate before forming opinions. When people discover facts that challenge their beliefs, they are disregarded altogether or, if acknowledged at all, they are held to a different standard of proof.

We are now seeing this post-truth influence play out to a greater degree in many areas of our society.

While we have the ability to feel emotions and emotions add color to our life, the foundation of our beliefs (including our religious beliefs) should always be truth, not emotions. Emotions come and go. Truth remains.

Scientism

Scientism has been defined as "excessive belief in the power of scientific knowledge and techniques."[7] Pbs.org had this to say about scientism: "In essence, scientism sees science as the absolute and only justifiable access to the truth."[8] Author Vince Vitale formerly embraced scientism.

> Without thinking it through, I jumped from science to scientism—from the fact that science can explain a lot to the assumption that it can explain everything. However, just because the advancement of science has taught us new things about how the universe works, that doesn't tell us whether there is a who behind the how.
>
> I can give you a full scientific explanation of how Microsoft Office works (well, I can't, but a computer expert could; he could sit you down with the design instructions for Microsoft Office and give you a full scientific explanation of how it works). But that would not show that Bill Gates doesn't exist; it wouldn't show that there is no who behind the how. To the contrary, it would show that Bill Gates is really smart!
>
> The how question (a question of mechanism) does not answer the who question (a question of agency), and it also doesn't answer the why question (a question of purpose): Why was Microsoft Office created? We can only get an answer to that question if Bill Gates chooses to share it with us, if the creator of the system chooses to reveal it. [9]

Additionally, not all claims widely accepted as scientific can be scientifically proven. Oxford scholar Dr. John Lennox noted, "The general public is not aware that not every statement by a scientist is necessarily a statement of science. And science has such cultural authority in our world that that confusion tends to exist."[10]

Scientific conclusions are not always based on empirical facts, but often on a combination of facts and opinions. As we know, opinions may or may not represent truth. One time that I personally experienced this scenario was during my cancer experience.

Two doctors from the same New Orleans area hospital had different opinions about the amount of chemotherapy I needed. One doctor was certain that I needed the lifetime limit of three different chemotherapy drugs. The other doctor let me know he would not *consider* giving me that much chemo. Both doctors based their medical opinions on science, had access to my medical records, and expressed total confidence in their very different opinions! I chose to go with more chemo rather than less and indications are that I needed all the chemo I was given. I may have had a very different outcome if I had believed the scientific opinion of the doctor who firmly recommended the lesser amount of chemotherapy. Although some science is considered "settled science," as this example illustrates, interpretations of scientific information can greatly differ.

Misinterpretation by highly respected scientists can also happen. In fact, Nobel Prize winner and Harvard University biologist Jack Szostak retracted some of the conclusions he made (which had furthered the theory of Darwinian evolution) after he realized he had misinterpreted the data. His mistaken conclusions were discovered when his colleague, Tivoli Olsen, tried to replicate the experiment. Szostak said, "In retrospect, we were totally blinded by our belief... we were not as careful or rigorous as we should have been (and as Tivoli was) in interpreting these experiments."[11] While interpretations by scientists can reflect the truth, based on human error and faulty speculation, sometimes their conclusions are incorrect.

Scientism also claims the human mind is an illusion because, according to scientism, nothing metaphysical is real—including our ability to reason. But it obviously takes a human mind to even make the claims that scientism makes. It takes a human mind to perform scientific methods and reach conclusions since everything cannot be scientifically tested. Some things must be reasoned. Therefore, interpretation by a human mind is necessary. To perceive, test, interpret and present scientific conclusions requires a mind—one that scientism denies exists.

Science is a very helpful tool, but not all realities can be determined through science.

"The truth will set you free." (John 8:32)

"Seek and you will find; knock and the door will be opened to you." (Matthew 7:7)

Truth is a treasure worthy of our deepest desires and passionate pursuit—especially when it comes to life's core questions. The more truth we know, the better. The more our life reflects the truth, the better off we are.

REASONS TO BELIEVE
GOD EXISTS

Earlier I shared my thought process when (over forty years ago) I concluded that God exists. I will now expound on my original thoughts and give some additional considerations for why it's reasonable to believe in the existence of the eternal, all-knowing, all-powerful, Supreme Being known as God.

THE EXISTENCE OF THE UNIVERSE

"The heavens declare the glory of God; the skies proclaim the work of his hands." (Psalm 19:1)

"For since the creation of the world God's invisible qualities—his eternal power and divine nature—have been clearly seen, being understood from what has been made." (Romans 1:20)

C. S. Lewis once said, "If there ever was a time that nothing existed, then nothing would exist now."[1] Reflect on that thought for a moment. But something does exist. We exist. Our universe exists.

Evidence for God surrounds us. All of creation is his masterpiece.

When we look at a painting, we know there was a painter who created it. We know there was a designer behind each article of clothing we own, the car we drive, and the computer we use. Every book we read had an author. Every song we play had a composer. Each person who has ever lived had a mother and father. With the same logic, it is reasonable to conclude that the universe had a Creator.

THE BEGINNING OF THE UNIVERSE

"In the beginning God created the heavens and the earth." (Genesis 1:1)

"The universe was formed at God's command, so that what is seen was not made out of what was visible." (Hebrews 11:3)

"Through him all things were made; without him nothing was made that has been made." (John 1:3)

I will present what I believe are the most plausible evidence-based explanations for the beginning of the universe, but first let's look at popular explanations within atheism.

In the *Evidence Bible*, author Ray Comfort notes a point that atheism has a difficult time defending.

> Many atheists refuse to admit they believe the entire universe came into being from nothing, because it is a scientific impossibility and they recognize how silly it sounds. If everything didn't come from nothing, their alternative is to say that creation (nature) created itself. However, a thing cannot make itself. To do so would mean that it had to pre-exist before it existed, and therefore it didn't create itself because it was already in existence.[2]

Although many who believe the universe came into being from nothing might not readily admit it, Richard Dawkins (an English biologist and author, and one of the most well-known atheists of our time) attempted to make that case. During a discussion with George Pell, the Catholic Cardinal of Sydney, Australia, Dawkins tried to define "nothing." Here is Dawkins' description of nothing:

> Of course, common sense doesn't allow you to get something from nothing. That's why it's interesting. It's got to be interesting in order to give rise to the universe at all. Something pretty mysterious had to give rise to the origin of the universe... You can dispute exactly what is meant by nothing, but whatever it is, it's very, very simple.[3]

At this point the audience broke into laughter, Dawkins turned to them and asked, "Why is that funny?" to which Cardinal Pell responded, "Well, I think it's a bit funny to be trying to define *nothing*."[4]

Other well-respected atheists have tried to defend how something could come from what they call "nothing," but their theories do not actually begin from the starting point of nothingness. They often base their theories on what is called a quantum vacuum. But a quantum vacuum is *something*—not nothing. A quantum vacuum can be described. It consists of fields of fluctuating energy. Any time we can describe what "nothing" is, it ceases to fit the definition of nothing. It is something.

Another popular theory to attempt to explain the origin of mankind without God's existence is that some form of alien life came to earth and deposited the original life form. In fact, Francis Crick, an outspoken atheist and Nobel Prize winner, discusses this theory of the origin of human life in his book, *Life Itself*. The theory he presents is that aliens from outer space who were more advanced than humans came to earth bringing with them some form of primordial life that (billions of years later) evolved into man.[5] However, no explanation is given for how these aliens came into existence.

I find it interesting that atheism will accept the possibility of a form of being they have never seen that is greater than man if this being is called "alien" but will reject a form of being greater than man who is called "God" because no one has seen God.

How did something come to exist?

More specifically, how did the "something" we call the universe begin? How did we get here? How could order in the universe have come from chaos? Could life have emerged from non-life? How could intangible attributes like consciousness, thoughts, emotions, and instincts have come only from physical matter—and where did that physical matter come from?

As noted previously, the night I became a Christian, I was at a place where I realized there are only three options for the source of all that exists. This universe was either created by man, by something or someone lesser than man (in intelligence and power), or by something or someone greater than man.

Man? Lesser than man? Greater than man? One of these options caused the existence of everything in our universe. One of these options is the reason that something rather than nothing exists.

Let's consider these options.

Obviously, no human is capable of creating a universe. I can't create a universe. You can't. Neither of us knows anyone who can. We humans also can't create anything else from nothing.

Is it then reasonable to believe that something or someone with *less* intelligence and power than man can create this universe? If man cannot create a universe, then how could something or someone with lesser capabilities than man create a universe? We are left with one other option:

Something or someone greater than man is responsible for the existence of our universe. I believe this is who the authors of the books of the Bible were describing when they referred to the eternal, all-knowing, all-powerful "Creator God."

We learn from Genesis that the universe did not always exist. At some point, it came into existence and God caused it to come into existence.

In the book, *I Don't Have Enough Faith to Be An Atheist*, Norman L. Geisler and Frank Turek wrote, "When you get right down to it, there are only two possibilities for anything that exists: either 1) it has always existed and is therefore uncaused, or 2) it had a beginning and was caused by something else"[6] Until the last few decades, most scientists believed the universe had always existed. But that is not the view of most scientists today. Most scientists believe our universe had a beginning. They claim overwhelming scientific evidence supports the theory that the universe came into existence in an instant (known as the "Big Bang Theory").

We know everything that comes into existence had a cause. If something did not previously exist and then it came into existence, something or someone caused it to come into existence. Therefore, if the universe is not eternal—if it had a beginning as most scientists now believe—something or someone pre-existed the universe and caused it to begin.

Scientists have not been able to explain the cause (often referred to as the "First Cause") of the instant explosion they believe resulted in the existence of our universe. Self-described agnostic and well-known astrophysicist Neil deGrasse Tyson admits it is "still unknown how [the universe] came into existence."[7] And here is how another scientist weighed in on this subject:

Robert Jastrow (1925-2008) was an astronomer, planetary physicist, and NASA scientist. During his career, he was the first chairman of the NASA Lunar Exploration Committee, Chief of NASA's Theoretical Division, and founding director of NASA's Goddard Institute for Space Studies. Jastrow was also a self-described agnostic. According to Wikipedia, "With the discovery of the Big Bang, Jastrow began to hold a belief that, if there was a beginning to the universe, there was also a Creator."[8]

In an interview with *Christianity Today*, Jastrow had this to say:

> Astronomers now find they have painted themselves into a corner because they have proven, by their own methods, that the world began abruptly in an act of creation to which you can trace the seeds of every star, every planet, every living thing in this cosmos and on the earth. And they have found that all this happened as a product of forces they cannot hope to discover... That there are what I or anyone would call super-natural forces at work is now, I think, a scientifically proven fact.[9]

In other words, even if we one day identify something from nature that set the Big Bang into motion, by having determined that the universe is not eternal—that it had a beginning, we would always be left with what remains unexplainable through natural causes: "Why is there something, rather than nothing?".

Jastrow also made the following comment in his book, *God and the Astronomers*:

> Now we see how the astronomical evidence supports the Biblical view of the origin of the world. The details differ, but the essential elements in the astronomical and Biblical accounts of Genesis are the same: the chain of events leading to man commenced suddenly and sharply at a definite moment in time, in a flash of light and energy.[10]

This was an interesting statement coming from an agnostic.

THE COMPLEXITY AND PRECISENESS OF CREATION

"There is for me powerful evidence that there is something going on behind it all… It seems as though somebody has fine-tuned nature's numbers to make the Universe... The impression of design is overwhelming."[11]
(Paul Davies, British Astrophysicist)

"We are, by astronomical standards, a pampered, cosseted, cherished group of creatures… If the Universe had not been made with the most exacting precision we could never have come into existence. It is my view that these circumstances indicate the universe was created for man to live in."[12]
(John O'Keefe, NASA Astronomer)

The universe is very complex and precise. According to NASA, in just our galaxy (the Milky Way) there are at least 100 billion planets and between 100-400 billion stars.[13] Our galaxy and the universe operate with extreme precision. Many conditions within our universe are interdependent and necessary for sustaining human life.

We find exacting precision not only at the extremely vast level of our galaxy and the universe, but also at the extremely small levels like the human body. We have more than twenty organs, some of which include our skin, brain, lungs, liver, kidneys, pancreas, stomach and heart. If one of these organs is not functioning properly it can impact other parts of our body. Our organs work together to sustain life and health. Evidence of design also exists in the microscopic parts of our bodies. Take our DNA, for example:

DNA

Often called the "book of life," a molecule known as DNA contains the instructions necessary for organisms to develop, live and reproduce. The complete set of an organism's DNA is called its *genome*. Genome.gov describes DNA this way:

> Deoxyribonucleic acid (DNA) is the chemical compound that contains the instructions needed to develop and direct the activities of nearly all living organisms. DNA molecules are made of two twisting, paired strands, often referred to as a double helix.
>
> Each DNA strand is made of four chemical units, called nucleotide bases, which comprise the genetic "alphabet." The bases are adenine (A), thymine (T), guanine (G), and cytosine (C)... The order of the As, Ts, Cs and Gs determines the meaning of the information encoded in that part of the DNA molecule just as the order of letters determines the meaning of a word...
>
> Virtually every single cell in the body contains a complete copy of the approximately 3 billion DNA base pairs, or letters, that make up the human genome. With its four-letter language, DNA contains the information needed to build the entire human body.[14]

It is incredible and almost incomprehensible to think about the fact that there are 3 billion DNA base pairs in *virtually every single cell* in our body! We find stunning detail and order in creation—from the smallest levels (such as DNA) to the vast universe. Stephen C. Meyer, philosopher of science and author of *Signature in the Cell,* made this comparison between DNA and computing:

> I think the digital revolution in computing has made it much easier to understand what's happening in biology. We know from experience that not only software but the information processing system and design strategies that software engineers use to process and store and utilize information are not only being used in digital computing but they're being used in the cell. It's the same basic design logic, but it's executed with an 8.0, 9.0, 10.0 efficiency. It's an elegance that far surpasses our own. It's a new day in biology. It's a digital revolution. We have digital nanotechnology running the show inside cells. It's exquisitely executed and suggests a preeminent mind.[15]

In 1990, the Human Genome Project began. The National Human Genome Research Institute described the project this way:

> The Human Genome Project (HGP) was one of the great feats of exploration in history… an international research effort to sequence and map all of the genes — together known as the genome—of members of our species, Homo sapiens. Completed in April 2003, the HGP gave us the ability, for the first time, to read nature's complete genetic blueprint for building a human being.[16]

The Director of this 13-year Human Genome Project was Dr. Francis S. Collins who headed up a team of over 1,000 scientists from six countries. This Human Genome Project was one of the most revolutionary scientific advancements of our time.

Here is how the DNA discoveries made in recent years impacted the beliefs of the late Antony Flew, a famous English philosopher and author of *There is a God—How the World's Most Notorious Atheist Changed His Mind:*

> I now believe there is a God... I now think [the evidence] does point to a creative Intelligence almost entirely because of the DNA investigations. What I think the DNA material has done is that it has shown, by the almost unbelievable complexity of the arrangements which are needed to produce life, that intelligence must have been involved in getting these extraordinarily diverse elements to work together.[17]

DNA is certainly compelling evidence that intelligence was used in creation.

Synthesizing proteins

Now, let me tell you about an interesting conversation I had approximately 20 years ago with my friend's sister-in-law about her work in synthesizing proteins.

Judith Ball has a Ph.D. in biochemistry. At the time we met she was an associate professor in the Department of Pathobiology at Texas A&M. During our conversation I learned that Judith is a Christian. I asked her how she reconciled science and God, when some working in science don't believe in God. She gave me one example from her personal experience, which I later asked her to put in writing. This is what she wrote:

> Proteins are made up of building blocks called amino acids. Small proteins include 50-100's of amino acids linked together (unique sequence of amino acids yields unique proteins), whereas large proteins are

composed of 1000's of amino acids. To synthesize a peptide (a small piece of a protein, usually about 20 amino acids) in the laboratory by chemically connecting the amino acids, it takes me and other scientists a minimum of a week if the process is automated. (To link one amino acid to another takes at least an hour.) The final peptide then has to be purified away from all the chemicals used in its synthesis and purified from any mistakes. Our body (in a single cell) can synthesize a large protein of 1000's of amino acids in microseconds! And this protein doesn't need purification.[18]

This is just one of the countless intricate processes that our bodies are designed to perform, and with incredible precision!

Signs of intelligence

Stephen C. Meyer makes this observation:

> We recognize intelligence all the time, and we have scientific methods for it. If you're an archaeologist and you're looking at the Rosetta Stone, are you duty-bound to continue looking for naturalistic explanations even though you know full well that wind and erosion and everything else you can imagine is not capable of making those inscriptions? No, you're not. You really ought to conclude the obvious, which is that a scribe was involved. There was an intelligence behind it.[19]

If we can look at the Rosetta Stone and know intelligence was behind the inscriptions carved into it, how can we look at everything in our universe, from DNA to the more than two trillion galaxies and not see an intelligence behind it all?

SCIENCE AND GOD – NOT INCOMPATIBLE AS SOME MIGHT THINK

Many people today assume that God and science are incompatible — that a person can either embrace science or God but not both. But is that true?

Here's how one of the foremost scientists today responded to this notion: "I am a scientist and a believer, and I find no conflict between those worldviews."[20]

Who made this statement? Francis S. Collins, the leader of the Human Genome Project mentioned previously. Collins is a Christian. He was an atheist until some conversations with patients during medical school motivated him to seek the truth. His search led him to belief in the God of the Bible and the claims of Jesus. Collins noted:

> I had always assumed that faith was based on purely emotional and irrational arguments, and was astounded to discover, initially in the writings of the Oxford scholar C. S. Lewis and subsequently from many other sources, that one could build a very strong case for the plausibility of the existence of God on purely rational grounds. My earlier atheist's assertion that "I know there is no God" emerged as the least defensible.[21]

In a statement Collins made, he confessed that his prior atheist views were not based on evidence:

> I had arrived at an answer to the most important issue that we humans ever deal with: "Is there a God?" And I had arrived there without ever really looking at the evidence. And I was supposed to be a scientist! If there is one thing scientists claim they do is to arrive at conclusions based upon evidence and I hadn't taken the trouble to do that.[22]

Collins describes his journey to investigate Christianity as a journey he was reluctant to begin, but felt he needed to. He said it was a journey he thought would result in strengthening his atheism but to his surprise it resulted in his conversion.[23] He has since authored books about God, science, and his Christian beliefs.

Also consider that the first scientist who suggested the Big Bang Theory was actually Georges Lemaitre—not Hubble. Lemaitre was a mathematician, an astronomer, professor of physics, *and* a Catholic priest. Wikipedia makes these comments about Lemaitre:

> He was the first to identify that the recession of nearby galaxies can be explained by a theory of an expanding universe, which was observationally confirmed soon afterwards by Edwin Hubble. He was the first to derive what used to be known as "Hubble's law", but since 2018 has officially been renamed the Hubble-Lemaitre law, and made the first estimation of what is still called the Hubble constant, which he published in 1927, two years before Hubble's article. Lemaitre also proposed what later became known as the "Big Bang theory" of the origin of the universe, initially calling it the "hypothesis of the primeval atom", and later calling it "the beginning of the world."[24]

Many other famous scientists through the years have expressed their belief in God. Here are quotes from a few:

- Joseph H. Taylor, Jr. received the 1993 Nobel Prize in Physics for the discovery of the first known binary pulsar, and for his work, which supported the Big Bang Theory of the creation of the universe. He said: "A scientific discovery is also a religious discovery. There is no conflict between science and religion. Our knowledge of God is made larger with every discovery we make about the world."[25]

48

- Louis Pasteur, famous 19th century biologist, microbiologist and chemist made this statement: "In good philosophy, the word 'cause' ought to be reserved to the single Divine impulse that has formed the universe... The more I study nature, the more I stand amazed at the work of the Creator."[26]

- Arthur L. Schawlow, Professor of Physics at Stanford University and recipient of the 1981 Nobel Prize in physics commented: "It seems to me that when confronted with the marvels of life and the universe, one must ask why and not just how. The only possible answers are religious... I find a need for God in the universe and in my own life."[27]

Science and belief in God are not incompatible as some might claim. According to the Religious Understandings of Science Study conducted by Sociologist Elaine Howard Ecklund in 2012-2014, "18 percent of scientists attended weekly religious services, compared with 20 percent of the general U.S. population and 15 percent consider themselves very religious (versus 19 percent of the general U. S. population)." Additionally, nearly "36 percent of scientists have no doubt about God's existence."[28]

What about evolution and the Big Bang Theory?

How are these theories viewed by Christians?

There are basically three responses to evolution within the Christian community. Some hold the position that the Darwinian theory of evolution is fully compatible with belief in God and the Bible. Other Christians do not believe this view of evolution is compatible with the Bible. And many Christians hold a view somewhere in-between. They accept micro-evolution (changes within a species), but not macro-evolution (changes from one species to another).

Differences of opinion also exist among Christians regarding the Big Bang Theory—some accepting this theory, others not accepting it.

Although there may be differing viewpoints by those who hold the Christian worldview about God's *process* of creation, Christians agree that God who is eternal, all-knowing and all-powerful is responsible for the creation of the universe and mankind.

MIND OR MATTER?

If minds are wholly dependent on brains, and brains on biochemistry, and biochemistry (in the long run) on the meaningless flux of the atoms, I cannot understand how the thought of these minds should have any more significance than the sound of the wind in the trees." [29] (C. S. Lewis)

John Lennox said, "The atheists' ultimate fact is the universe; the theist's ultimate fact is God. That is the burning question: In which direction does science point—matter before mind or mind before matter?"[30] Was matter behind the creation of the mind, or was mind behind the creation of matter?

But how could mindless matter create something much more complex than itself (the human mind, for example)? How could mindless matter program our bodies to perform their intricate functions? How could mindless matter program the universe to operate as it does? These factors would be necessary to support the theory that matter created everything. Even so, we would still be left with the question of how matter came into existence in the first place, since it is widely accepted that matter didn't eternally exist. (As noted earlier in the quote by Ray Comfort, "a thing cannot make itself. To do so would mean that it had to pre-exist before it existed, and therefore it didn't create itself because it was already in existence.")

Christianity teaches that we and our universe were conceived in the mind of God who is eternal, all-knowing and all-powerful.. God wanted us to exist and he willed us into existence. He created our universe and he created us.

Is it more reasonable to believe that we and the entire universe are the result of mindless matter or that an intelligence (a mind) is behind all of creation? Mind or matter? I believe the evidence is overwhelmingly in favor of *mind*—the mind of the Supreme Being we know as God.

Since something cannot come from nothing, this means our Creator existed before our universe existed. The evidence in our world and beyond is clear. It certainly required more power and intelligence than we possess for the creation of all that exists. Our Creator is eternal, exists in a dimension of reality we are not capable of fully comprehending, and has a power and intelligence beyond our human abilities. This description of our Creator is consistent with the description of the God of the Bible.

REASONS TO BELIEVE
THE BIBLE IS RELIABLE

"For the word of the LORD is right and true." (Psalm 33:4)

"Your word is a lamp for my feet, a light on my path." (Psalm 119:105)

"The grass withers and the flowers fall, but the word of our God endures forever." (Isaiah 40:8)

In his book, *Loving God*, Charles W. Colson made the following statement about the Bible:

> The Bible—banned, burned, beloved. More widely read, more frequently attacked than any other book in history. Generations of intellectuals have attempted to discredit it; dictators of every age have outlawed it and executed those who read it. Yet... [f]ragments of it smuggled into solitary prison cells have transformed ruthless killers into gentle saints.[1]

No book has impacted mankind more than the book we know as the Bible.

What makes this book unique? Why can we trust it?

THE BIBLE AND ITS ORIGIN

With an estimated 5 *billion* copies in print, the Bible (sometimes called "God's Word," and "Holy Scriptures") is the best-selling and most widely distributed book in the history of the world. The Bible was also the first book ever printed after the mid-fifteenth century invention of Gutenberg's printing press. According to Wycliffe Global Alliance,

3,384 languages have either portions of the Bible or the entire Bible, making it the most translated book in history.[2]

The Bible is a compilation of many books, 66 recognized by most Christian faiths and an additional 7 recognized by the Catholic Church. These books are grouped together into two parts: the Old Testament and the New Testament. The Old Testament books were written before Jesus' birth—some of them were written over 1000 years earlier. The New Testament books cover the period beginning with the birth of Jesus and they were written within a range of about 35-100 years after his death (some scholars estimate the dates to be slightly earlier, some later). The Bible was not originally written in chapters and verses. In the early thirteenth century it was divided into chapters to find specific scriptures more easily. Within the next few centuries, the chapters were divided into verses (sometimes called "passages").

These books represent many different literary genres. The books of the Bible were written by about 40 authors on three different continents (Asia, Africa, and Europe) in three languages (Hebrew, Greek and Aramaic) during a period of about 1,500 years in the midst of different settings from royal palaces to prison. The authors were also from many different walks of life and include a fisherman, physician, tax collector, tent maker, royal cupbearer, shepherd, military men, and kings.

GOD INSPIRED

The Bible is the foremost way God has chosen to communicate to us today. It is not the only way but the primary way. Through the Bible, God answers the compelling questions we desire to understand: the origin of the universe and man; who we are; the meaning and purpose of our life; how we can live out our purpose; and what happens to us when we die. Through the Bible we also learn what God is like and many other truths he has chosen to reveal to us.

We read in 2 Timothy 3:16-17, "All Scripture is God-breathed and is useful for teaching, rebuking, correcting and training in righteousness, so that the servant of God may be thoroughly equipped for every good work."

The term "God-breathed" is also translated as "God-inspired," which means that although the books of the Bible were written by human authors, they were inspired by God.

What does "God-inspired" mean? Some think it means God dictated word-for-word what the authors should write. Others believe God inspired the authors who then wrote in their own styles and through their own personalities the thoughts that God had given them. Biblica (The International Bible Society) says "most Christians conclude that God provided the precise thought to the human author, and he then wrote it down in terms of his own vocabulary, culture, education, and writing style."[3]

Biblica makes this observation: "First of all, as we look at the writing styles of the various human authors, it is clear that their personalities are very much in evidence in what they write. There is no mechanical word-for-word dictation going on here."[4]

Another reason Biblica gives for why a word-for-word dictation is not likely is that "many of the Psalms (and other passages) are the cries of imperfect, suffering people, who are voicing their own complaints or praises to God. They are words and thoughts emanating directly from the hearts of God's people…"[5] Biblica goes on to say:

> For those reasons many Christians believe that inspiration should be described as thought-for-thought rather than word-for-word. The human writers provide God's message in terms of their own personalities and historical circumstances, and yet they transmit the message fully and exactly as God desired. So we can call this view of inspiration "dynamic," as well as "verbal" (extending to the very words of the writer) and "plenary" (meaning that the Bible is fully and totally inspired.)… [W]e can say that the Bible is a

very human book, for we see in it both elegance and lack of polish, both finesse and struggle. But it is a divine book as well, for it is the only book in all the world that is truly "God-breathed." It is humanity's precious gift from God.[6]

The words of the Bible are not only inspired by God, but they can also inform and inspire each of us.

Let us now consider reasons we can trust that the Bible is reliable. There are three common ways used to authenticate the reliability of all ancient documents and books—the bibliographical test, the internal test, and the external test. We use these same tests to authenticate the reliability of the Bible.

BIBLIOGRAPHICAL EVIDENCE

The bibliographical test examines how accurately ancient documents have been transmitted through the years. This test requires knowing the following factors: the date the work was originally written, the date of the earliest known existing manuscript, and the number of known manuscripts. Manuscripts may include a complete written work, parts of a written work, or even a small fragment of a written work. According to Daniel B. Wallace, Executive Director of the Center for the Study of New Testament Manuscripts, "the average size for a [New Testament] manuscript is more than 450 pages."[7] With ancient literature (especially works written thousands of years ago), we are usually working with manuscripts that were copied from the original, not the original itself. This is also true of the Bible.

The time gap between when written and the earliest manuscript

By knowing the date an ancient work was written (i.e., the original or "autograph") and the date of the earliest known existing manuscript, we can calculate the time gap between the two. The fewer years between the date the work was written and the earliest manuscript the more accurate (in most cases) the manuscript is likely to be.

How does the Bible stack up against the classical literature we readily accept as authentic and reliable? With classical literature, a time gap of 500-1,000 years between when a work was originally written and the earliest known manuscript is not uncommon. Compare this to the earliest New Testament manuscript with a gap of about 100 years!

The number of manuscripts

Let's now compare the number of manuscripts between the Greek New Testament and the manuscripts of other ancient literature. Presumably, the greater number of manuscripts, the better. More manuscripts allow for more comparison of the texts, providing a greater degree of "checks and balances" in determining authenticity.

Regarding classical texts, rarely will we have more than a couple hundred manuscripts—often, much less. So, how many Greek New Testament manuscripts do we have? Over 5,000. In addition to the 5,000+ Greek New Testament manuscripts, we have about 20,000 ancient manuscripts of New Testament versions including Latin, Coptic, Syriac, and other versions.

As you can see, no other ancient work comes close to the Bible regarding the number of manuscripts.

Did the scribes accurately copy the Bible?

Does saying the Bible has been "reliably transmitted through the ages" mean the thousands of manuscripts were perfectly transcribed?

Until the mid-fifteen century when the printing press began, copying the Bible meant copying by hand. While Christianity holds that the books of the Bible (the *original* manuscripts) are "inerrant," meaning they're without mistakes, what about the thousands of manuscripts that have been copied by scribes through the centuries? Do they all match letter-for-letter, or are there any differences between them?

Differences, called "variants," exist in the copied manuscripts, but variants are not unique to the Bible. They also appear in other ancient works.

Peter Gurry, PhD. estimates about 500,000 Greek New Testament variants, not including spelling errors.[8] Of course, this is not in a *single* manuscript; the total refers to *all* of the manuscripts. This number might sound excessive... until we consider three important factors.

First, we have over five thousand Greek New Testament manuscripts. Dr. Daniel B. Wallace commented that "[t]he reason we have a lot of variants is that we have a lot of manuscripts. To speak about the number of variants without also speaking about the number of manuscripts is simply an appeal to sensationalism."[9]

Second, we must consider what counts as a variant. Let's look at the four categories of variants outlined in Wallace's book, *Reinventing Jesus: What the Da Vinci Code and Other Novel Speculations Don't Tell You* (co-authored with Komoszewski and Sawyer). The categories are listed from the largest percentage to the lowest percentage of variants:

"Spelling errors" (not included in the previously mentioned estimate)

Dr. Wallace points out that "at least 75% of all variants" consist of misspellings or, in some cases, what appears to be a very minor mistake because a scribe was likely fatigued or inattentive.[10]

"Variants that do not affect translation"

Synonyms are one example Dr. Wallace gives of this type of variant. In another example he explains that word order "is very flexible" in the Greek language. Sometimes the word order is changed but the same thought is still expressed. He notes that "[f]or the most part, the only difference is one of emphasis, not meaning."[11]

"Meaningful, but not viable variants"

To explain this category of variants, Wallace gives the following example:

[I]n Luke 6:22, the ESV reads, "Blessed are you when people hate you and when they exclude you and revile you and spurn your name as evil, on account of the Son of Man!" But one manuscript from the 10th/11th century (codex 2882) lacks the words, "on account of the Son of Man." That's a very meaningful variant since it seems to say that a person is blessed when he is persecuted, regardless of his allegiance to Christ. Yet it is only in one manuscript, and a relatively late one at that. It has no chance of reflecting the wording of the original text, since all the other manuscripts are against it, including quite a few that are much, much earlier.[12]

"Meaningful and viable variants"

In this category, Dr. Wallace notes that this type of variant changes the meaning of the text "to some degree." This does not necessarily indicate that the change of meaning is significant. Wallace points out that this category comprises the smallest number of variants – "less than 1% of all textual variants."[13]

The third, most important factor to consider is that none of the variants, including those that are meaningful and viable, have impacted any of the core beliefs of Christianity. Let's look at what some scholars of New Testament textual research have to say about this. ("Textual critic" is the formal title for these researchers. I will use this term and the word "critic" several times in this book. To clarify, the word "critic" as used here does not indicate negative criticism of the text. It simply refers to those who are researching and critiquing the text.)

Dr. Daniel Wallace:

Dr. Wallace says that of the "less than 1%" of variants that are meaningful and viable, "no cardinal belief is at stake."[14]

Dr. Norman Geisler

Christian theologian and philosopher, Dr. Norman Geisler, sums up variants and bibliographical tests this way:

> Not only are there more and earlier [New Testament] manuscripts, but also they were more accurately copied than any other ancient texts. The NT scholar and Princeton professor (the late) Bruce Metzger made a comparison of the NT with the Iliad of Homer and the Mahabharata of Hinduism. He found the text of the latter to represent only 90 percent of the original (with 10 percent textual corruption), the Iliad to be 95 percent pure, and only half of 1 percent of the NT text to remain in doubt.[15]

Dr. Bart Ehrman:

New Testament textual critics who are Christians aren't the only ones who hold the position that the variants do not impact core Christian beliefs. Bart Ehrman, a textual critic and self-described agnostic-atheist, said in an interview that his position (about whether or not the variants impact Christian beliefs) "does not actually stand at odds with Prof. Metzger's position that the essential Christian beliefs are not affected by textual variants in the manuscript tradition of the New Testament."[16]

What happens when a text is in question or scholars agree to make a change due to variants? In some cases, when a Bible verse is still in question, critics may mark it with a footnote explaining the circumstances around that text. In rare cases, if scholars widely accept that making a change would more likely reflect what the authors originally wrote, then a change would be made. But it is very seldom necessary to change anything in the Bible. As mentioned previously, scholars may find minor changes as they study the manuscripts (from misspellings to a change in word order, and other insignificant changes), but any variants more significant than that are extremely rare. Because of the great amount of manuscript evidence, the biblical text we have has been stable and reliable over time.

INTERNAL EVIDENCE

The internal test considers evidence *within* the Bible. Are the authors believable? Is there consistency in what was written within?

The short answer to both questions is "yes." An explanation of why we can be confident that the authors are believable is in the next chapter ("Reasons to Believe the Claims of Jesus"). Now, let's look at where the Bible stands regarding consistency.

The Bible presents a cohesive story consistent in its main themes and messages: the creation of the universe and man; the characteristics of God; the nature of man; the fall of man; and the redemption of man, to name a few. The consistency throughout the 60+ books of the Bible is remarkable when one considers the very inconsistent circumstances in which the books of the Bible were written. To summarize what was noted earlier, there were about forty or more authors with diverse backgrounds from three continents. These books were written in three different languages over a period of about 1,500 years in various settings, yet the authors record consistent themes and messages.

We find great consistency not only in the main messages of the books of the Bible, but also in the details when we understand a passage in its context. The principle of applying context (or "contextualizing") is not unique to the Bible. Applying context is necessary for an accurate understanding of all ancient and contemporary documents and books.

We can categorize the different types of context by literary genre, linguistic, textual and historical. An explanation follows of each of these contexts with regard to the Bible:

Literary genre context

There are many different literary genres in the Bible, such as history, laws, genealogies, wisdom, prophecies, songs, poetry, prayers, letters (also known as "epistles"), and parables.

Robert Stewart, Professor of Philosophy and Theology at New Orleans Baptist Theological Seminary, said, "If we read every book of the Bible like every other book of the Bible, we will be misreading the Bible, just like we would be misreading Moby Dick if we read it like we read the dictionary or a map or a modern poem."[17]

Here are three examples of literary genres found in the Bible and the need to interpret them in context:

Letters

Some of the letters in the Bible were meant only for a particular audience and purpose—usually to address a specific problem, need or question. Other letters were more general, applying to the church as a whole. Understanding who the author was writing to is necessary to understand the context.

Parables

Parables are simple fictitious stories used to illustrate a lesson or truth. Parables were one of Jesus' favorite genres to use. Over thirty parables told by Jesus are recorded in the New Testament. Parables are meant to be taken figuratively, not literally. Taking parables literally would be incorrectly interpreting them.

Laws

There are over 600 laws in the Old Testament: "ceremonial laws" (laws pertaining to ceremonial systems in place prior to Jesus' sacrifice on the cross), "civil laws" (laws that were specifically for the people of ancient Israel), and "moral laws." Some overlap exists between the civil laws given to ancient Israel and the moral laws. We would be misunderstanding the Scriptures if we think all or none of these Old Testament laws apply to us today.

Linguistic context

Linguistic context is considering what the words meant at the time they were written, not what they mean today. At times the meaning of words and phrases used then and now will be the same. In other cases, today's meaning of the word is different (even very different) from what the word meant in biblical times.

In my lifetime, the meaning of some words and phrases have changed. A few years ago, I used a common phrase when talking with my daughter. She responded, "Mom, you cannot say that anymore!" She told me the phrase has a new meaning that infers something off-color. The change in the meaning of that phrase took place in the span of one generation. How much more can the meaning of words and phrases change in a few thousand years? To avoid misinterpreting the Bible, we need to know what the author's words meant at the time they were written. Here are some biblical examples:

Idioms

Idioms are phrases not intended to be literal, and idioms are sometimes used in the Bible. Interestingly, more than a hundred commonly used idioms today in the American culture originated from the Bible. If you've ever said any of the following, you've quoted the Bible.

- a drop in the bucket
- bite the dust
- peace offering
- the blind leading the blind
- Can a leopard change his spots?
- go the extra mile
- nothing but skin and bones
- the powers that be
- put words in one's mouth
- rise and shine
- see eye to eye
- sign of the times

Although we are familiar with many of these idioms, some idioms and phrases used in biblical times are not common today. If we don't realize we are reading an idiom and we take the words literally, we will misinterpret what the author meant to communicate. For instance, if years from now people read the idiom we currently use, "he let the cat out of the bag," and take those words literally, they would be misinterpreting what we meant to communicate.

Here is an example of an idiom used in the Bible that has been misrepresented:

In a few places, the Bible refers to the four corners of the earth. Some have mistaken this to mean that the Bible suggests the earth is flat. However, that is not what this idiom meant. It was used in that day in the same way we now use the phrase "to the ends of the earth." We don't really think there is a physical *end* of the earth. At the time these biblical passages were written, this term, "four corners of the earth" or "corners of the earth" meant "all of the earth" or the four cardinal directions—north, south, east, and west. It was not meant literally.

The meaning of words

The meaning of a single word can also change through the years. Some words were defined differently in biblical times than they are today. We need to understand what specific words meant to correctly interpret what we're reading.

David Murray gives us a modern-day example of this scenario:

> [I]f you're fishing in a boat and someone says, "Will you get off the net?" you look around your feet to see if you are standing on the landing net. But if you're sitting at a computer and Dad says to you, "Will you get off the net?" you're looking for the "Close Browser" button. Same word, but different surroundings make the word mean something completely different.[18]

Some words used in the Bible had more than one meaning when they were written but have a singular meaning today. We may assume that those words in the Bible we are familiar with meant then what they mean today, but that is not always the case. Applying today's meaning to a word may, or may not, be correct.

"Fear" is an example of a word used in the Bible that in biblical times had more than one meaning. We are told over and over in the Bible not to fear, yet the Bible also tells us to fear God. Without context, this seems like a contradiction. Today the word fear means "to be afraid." But let's delve into the Hebrew and Greek words for fear used in biblical times. The Hebrew word for fear is *yare* and this word had several meanings: "be afraid," "revere," "awe" and "respect."[19] The Greek word for fear is *phobeo* and it meant "to fear" or "to reverence."[20] This is why context is important. In some places in the Bible where the translated word is fear, today's definition of the word is applicable. However, other times in the Bible, the obvious meaning of the word is reverence or awe.

Hyperbole and metaphors

Linguistic context is also needed with regard to hyperbole and metaphors.

Hyperbole is exaggeration to make a point, but is not to be taken literally. In biblical days, as is the case today, hyperbole is sometimes used in statements. If I were to say, "*Everyone* is going to the party," or, "I have a *million* errands to run," this would be hyperbole. We can find hyperbole in the Old and New Testaments as well. Jesus used hyperbole, too. For example: "But when you give to the needy, do not let your left hand know what your right hand is doing," (Matthew 6:3)

A metaphor is when a word or phrase is compared to something or some action to present an analogy between the two. In John 10:7 Jesus described himself as "the gate for the sheep." He was not claiming to be a literal gate for literal sheep, but rather that he is the entryway for mankind.

Textual context

Context applied within verses and between verses is considered textual context. Let's look at some examples of the need to apply textual context to biblical texts.

Example: context within a verse

Did you know the Bible says, "There is no God"? Yep! These exact words are in the Bible—in Psalm 14:1. You might be thinking, "Wait a minute—we just spent a whole chapter about the Bible's claim that God exists!" But, let's read these words in context with the rest of the verse: "The fool says in his heart, 'There is no God'" So, technically, the statement "There is no God" is in the Bible, but you can see how taking words out of context can totally change the meaning.

Example: context with surrounding verses

Here is an example of context with surrounding verses: A popular verse reads "I can do all things through him who strengthens me" (Philippians 4:13 ESV). We could easily take this verse (especially the words "all things") out of context and assign a meaning to it the author did not intend. Does "all things" mean I can do anything I imagine? Can I fly as a bird flies? Can I walk through a wall? When we read this verse in context with the surrounding verses, we will better understand what Paul was communicating. He was discussing the need not only to be content in the good times, but also in the hard times. "All things" in this context refers to enduring whatever difficult circumstances and hardships we encounter in the process of serving Christ.

Historical context

Historical context takes into account the cultural conditions at the time and location of the author, such as social, economic, religious and political events and practices. Knowing the historical context of the Scriptures gives us the backdrop and the deeper meanings behind the text.

For example, at the last supper Jesus had with the apostles before his capture and crucifixion, he washed their feet. This was a custom in Hebrew homes that was extended to guests. The lowliest of servants usually performed this act. Understanding this custom helps put in context what Jesus intended to convey. Washing the apostle's feet was an expression and illustration of what Jesus had said in other settings: that he did not come to be served but to serve and to give his life as a ransom for many. In this act (as in other acts) Jesus put himself in the lowliest position to serve others.

EXTERNAL EVIDENCE

What external (archaeological) evidence is there for the Bible?

J. Warner Wallace is a well-known homicide detective, expert on evidence, former atheist, and Christian apologist. He makes this statement in an article titled, "Verifiability is a Christian Distinctive":

> Some religious systems are based purely on the doctrinal, proverbial statements of their founders. The wisdom statements of Buddha, for example, lay the foundation for Buddhism. In a similar way, the statements of L. Ron Hubbard for the basis of Scientology. But in both these examples, the statements of these worldview leaders exist independently of any event in history. In other words, these systems rise or fall on the basis of ideas and concepts, rather than on claims about a particular historical event.[21]

Although Christianity includes ideas and concepts, it hinges on the historical event of the resurrection of Jesus. (Evidence for the resurrection is covered in the next chapter.) The Bible also contains many other historical people, events, and details. We can put these claims to the same tests we use to authenticate all other historical claims. Through the years, archaeology has validated thousands of biblical claims from minor details to major events.

Examples of archaeological evidence for the Bible

The following are examples of external evidence for the Bible (as reported by various scholars).

Sheri Bell: "Archaeology Helps to Confirm the Historicity of the Bible"

Archeology has absolutely confirmed historical detail that Luke included in his Gospel. Luke's primary focus in this book is meticulously showcasing who Jesus was—and what He came to do. He did so with facts, not fanciful detail.

At one time, however, scholars thought that Luke had entirely missed the boat regarding the events surrounding the birth of Jesus (Luke 2:1-3). Critics argued that there was no census, that Quirinius was not governor of Syria at that time, and that everyone did not have to return to his ancestral home. But archeological discoveries show that the Romans had a regular enrollment of taxpayers and also held censuses every fourteen years. This procedure began under Augustus. Further, we find that Quirinius was, indeed, governor of Syria around 7 BC. It is supposed that he was governor twice, once in 7 BC and again in AD 6 (the date ascribed by Josephus.) [NOTE: Josephus was not a biblical author, but a first century historian.] A papyrus found in Egypt gives directions for the conduct of a census.

Concerning Luke's ability as a historian, Sir William Mitchell Ramsey, one of the greatest archeologists to have ever lived, said, after 30 years of study, that, "Luke is a historian of the first rank; not merely are his statements of fact trustworthy... this author should be placed along with the greatest of historians."[22]

<u>John Stonestreet and Roberto Rivera: "The Reliability of
Scripture: That Which We Have Seen With Our Eyes"</u>

Paul tells the Corinthians, in 2 Corinthians 11, that "At
Damascus, the governor under King Aretas was
guarding the city of Damascus in order to seize me."
Aretas, "a contemporary of Herod Antipas," was a real
person whose existence has been documented by both
extra-biblical sources and archaeology. Coins and other
artifacts bearing his name have been found from
what's now Jordan to Italy. What we know of his life
and reign outside of the Bible argues for the historicity
of Paul's account.[23]

<u>J. Warner Wallace: "A Brief Sample of Old Testament
Archaeological Corroboration"</u>

The historicity of the Assyrian king, Sargon (recorded
in Isaiah 20:1) has also been confirmed, in spite of the
fact his name was not seen in any non-Biblical record.
Archeology again proved the Biblical account to be true
when Sargon's palace was discovered in Khorsabad,
Iraq. More importantly, the event mentioned in Isaiah
20, Sargon's capture of Ashdod, was recorded on the
palace walls, confirming the history recorded in Old
Testament Scripture. Fragments of a stela (an inscribed
stone pillar) were also found at Ashdod. This stela was
originally carved to memorialize the victory of
Sargon.[24]

These are just a few examples of archaeological discoveries that
have validated biblical accounts. If you are interested in more
information on biblical archaeological discoveries, see "Resources" on
my website (heartforgod.org).

A few notes on biblical discoveries through archaeology

At times I've seen news reports present wrong conclusions about the Bible after archaeological discoveries.

For example, in mid-2017 numerous news reports claimed the Bible taught that the Canaanite population had been annihilated but that DNA testing had proved the Canaanite population had *not* been annihilated. They claimed this DNA finding disproved the biblical account about the Canaanites. But then an article titled "Canaanite DNA and the Biblical Canon" by Dr. Dewayne Bryant was published. Bryant explained how reporters were wrong in their understanding of what the Bible says. The Bible tells us that an *attempt* was made to eliminate the Canaanites, but later says that this effort was not completed. The Bible did not say the entire Canaanite population was annihilated as some had reported. To the contrary, it confirms they were not. Dr. Bryant then went into detail explaining how, as he puts it, "Far from undermining the biblical text, the most recent findings concerning Canaanite DNA support the accuracy of Scripture."[25]

The conclusion by some that this DNA evidence disproved a biblical account was not factual. Nevertheless, well-respected sources circulated news reports that this DNA discovery had disproved the Bible. I wonder how many people read those reports and took what they read at face value.

Based on our post-truth culture, we can likely expect more misreporting in the future. When we see news reports claiming an archaeological discovery has disproved something in the Bible, I suggest we don't automatically accept these reports as factual. People with more biblical knowledge will usually respond (on the internet where it is easily accessible) and correct misinformation within a few days.

Additionally, in several of the archaeological examples noted earlier, prior to these discoveries there were firm opinions held by some archaeologists that the biblical account was not accurate. But then *new* archaeological discoveries confirmed the biblical accounts.

So, even when scholars make claims challenging biblical accounts, it's possible that future discoveries will prove otherwise. After all, although thousands of discoveries validating biblical accounts have already been made, archaeologists say only a very small fraction of what is discoverable in the world through archaeology has been found.

What about evidence for reports of miracles that are recorded in the Bible? The following is from the josh.org article, "Does Archaeological Evidence Prove the Bible?".

> Although the miracles recorded in Scripture cannot be scientifically tested or repeated due to their nature, persons, places, and events can be investigated historically. If the biblical writers were incorrect in their historical picture, serious doubt would then be cast upon their trustworthiness in areas which couldn't be verified.
>
> Putting it another way, if the authors of Scripture are accurate in their accounts of the things that transpired, it then follows that they cannot be ruled out of court because they happen to mention things out of the ordinary.[26]

Speaking of miracles, I offer this food for thought: I realize some may question whether miracles, specifically those mentioned in the Bible, are even possible. But let's think about this in the context of belief in God's existence. If God has already performed the biggest miracle of all time (i.e., creation), then would performing what we call a miracle within that creation be something out of the realm of possibilities for him? Of course not! So, in the framework of a worldview in which God exists, miracles are certainly and logically possible.

The Bible is the most unique book in the history of the world, and the number of lives it has touched through the ages is immeasurable! In all of the methods and standards we use to validate any historical document (bibliographical, internal and external tests), the Bible excels. If we accept *any* historical document or book as being reliable, then by the same standards, we must conclude that the Bible is also reliable.

I will close this chapter with a quote that has circulated for many years by an unknown author describing the Bible:

> *The Bible contains the mind of God, the state of man, the way of salvation, the doom of sinners and the happiness of believers. Its doctrines are holy, its precepts are binding, its histories are true, and its decisions are immutable. Read it to be wise, believe it to be safe and practice it to be holy. It contains light to direct you, food to support you and comfort to cheer you. It is the traveler's map, the pilgrim's staff, the pilot's compass, the soldier's sword and the Christian's character. Here paradise is restored, heaven opened and the gates of hell disclosed. Christ is its grand object, our good is its design and the glory of God its end. It should fill the memory, rule the heart, and guide the feet. Read it slowly, frequently, and prayerfully.*

REASONS TO BELIEVE
THE CLAIMS OF JESUS

I was probably in my twenties the first time I read "One Solitary Life" by Dr. James Allen Francis (1864-1928). A paraphrased version of this selection was on a Christmas card I received. It is still a favorite of mine.

> Here is a man who was born in an obscure village, the child of a peasant woman. He grew up in another obscure village, where He worked in a carpenter shop until He was thirty, and then for three years He was an itinerant preacher. He never wrote a book. He never held an office. He never owned a home. He never had a family. He never went to college. He never put his foot inside a big city. He never traveled two hundred miles from the place where He was born. He never did one of the things that usually accompany greatness. He had no credentials but Himself. While still a young man, the tide of public opinion turned against Him. His friends ran away. One of them denied Him. He was turned over to His enemies. He went through the mockery of a trial. He was nailed to a cross between two thieves. His executioners gambled for the only piece of property He had on earth while He was dying—and that was his coat. When he was dead He was taken down and laid in a borrowed grave through the pity of a friend. Nineteen wide centuries have come and gone and today He is the centerpiece of the human race. I am far within the mark when I say that all the armies that ever

marched, and all the navies that ever were built, and all the parliaments that ever sat, all the kings that ever reigned, put together have not affected the life of man upon this earth as powerfully as has that One Solitary Life.[1]

Jesus walked this earth a little over 2000 years ago. The authors of the New Testament books and others outside of any religious context, like first and second-century historians, recorded his life. In his short ministry lasting about three years Jesus started a movement we know as Christianity. The unmatched influence of Jesus continues today.

Jesus is the founder of Christianity, yet other major religions like Islam, Baha'i, Hinduism, Buddhism and New Age also acknowledge Jesus. These religions do not view Jesus the same way he is viewed within Christianity. Some consider Jesus to be a good teacher, a prophet or a good example. Nevertheless, the fact that so many major world religions acknowledge Jesus shows his widespread and lasting impact.

The question is... *why*? What was so different about this "one solitary life?"

Where does one look for answers to these and other questions about Jesus? J. Warner Wallace offers the following:

Given Jesus is a common feature of the major religions of the world, it might be important for us to learn more about the man whom everyone feels the need to describe. While the world's religions account for Jesus tangentially, only one faith system is established on the authentic, attested eyewitness accounts of Jesus' life, teaching and ministry. If one was inclined to begin a spiritual quest for truth, it would be wise to start with the faith system best describing the man all other faith systems find themselves compelled to explain.[2]

In this chapter we will look at the life of Jesus: who he is, what he claimed, and why his claims are believable.

WHO IS JESUS?

Jesus – A Historical Figure

I shared at the beginning of this book that my history professor decades ago said Jesus was just a myth. With vast evidence to the contrary, it is surprising that this assertion still surfaces from time to time.

Respected scholars and historians today with and without religious backgrounds and non-Christians alike overwhelmingly accept Jesus as a historical figure.

Jesus was born about 6-4BC and died approximately 30AD. One may wonder about the timing of Jesus' birth because BC stands for "before Christ." The use of BC and AD in Gregorian and Julian calendars was implemented around 500AD to make the birth of Jesus the event that separates history. As for Jesus' birth year being a few years BC, and not 1AD (as one would expect), this is the result of a miscalculation that was made about the actual year of Jesus' birth when the calendar was originally set up. Also, AD is often misunderstood as an abbreviation for "after the death" of Jesus. However, "AD" stands for "anno domini" which means "in the year of the Lord."

Evidence in support of Jesus' existence comes very soon after the time of his death. We have sources from some who were his followers and others who were not. For now, we will address evidence from some who were *not* followers of Jesus, and later in this chapter we'll look at some of the evidence presented by his followers.

Reports about Jesus from non-Christian sources

J. Warner Wallace notes some "reluctant admissions" about Jesus by early non-Christian sources.

Josephus (37-101AD)

Even when examining the modest, redacted version of Josephus' ancient account, it's clear that this Jewish historian reluctantly affirmed the following: Jesus lived in Palestine, was a wise man and a teacher, worked amazing deeds, was accused by the Jews, crucified under Pilate and had followers called Christians.

Thallus (52AD)

While Thallus appeared to deny the supernatural aspect of the gospel narratives, he did reluctantly repeat and affirm the following: Jesus lived, was crucified, and there was an earthquake and darkness at the point of his crucifixion.

Tacitus (56-120AD)

Cornelius Tacitus (known for his analysis and examination of historical documents and among the most trusted of ancient historians) described Nero's response to the great fire in Rome and reluctantly affirmed the following: Jesus lived in Judea, was crucified under Pontius Pilate, and had followers who were persecuted for their faith in Christ.

Mara Bar-Serapion (70AD)

Sometime after 70AD, this Syrian philosopher, writing to encourage his son, compared the life and persecution of Jesus with that of other philosophers who were persecuted and reluctantly affirmed the following: Jesus was a wise and influential man who died for his beliefs, His followers adopted these beliefs and lived lives that reflected them.

Phlegon (80-140AD)

Phlegon wrote a chronicle of history around 140AD and reluctantly affirmed the following details about

Jesus: Jesus had the ability to accurately predict the future, was crucified under the reign of Tiberius Caesar and demonstrated his wounds after he was resurrected.[3]

Simon Gathercole, New Testament scholar at Cambridge University, shares the following.

Strikingly, there was never any debate in the ancient world about whether Jesus of Nazareth was a historical figure. In the earliest literature of the Jewish Rabbis, Jesus was denounced as the illegitimate child of Mary and a sorcerer. Among pagans, the satirist Lucian and philosopher Celsus dismissed Jesus as a scoundrel, but we know of no one in the ancient world who questioned whether Jesus lived.[4]

Not only do we have zero evidence of any ancient claims that Jesus did not exist, but the previous references show historians, politicians, and others who lived near the time of Jesus make references consistent with what we read about him in biblical accounts. The fact that we have historical accounts of Jesus by some who were obviously not his fans only strengthens the case for Jesus as a historical figure.

Jesus – the meaning of his name

In biblical times, names held more significance than they do now. Parents today often choose the name of their child because they like a name or the way it sounds with his or her surname. That is not how a child's name was chosen in biblical times. Names chosen were intentionally descriptive—revealing some aspect of a person's identity, traits, physical characteristics, nature, association, or destiny.

The name Jesus means "God saves," conveying both Jesus' identity and mission. Writers communicate throughout the Bible that

God consists of three persons: Father, Son and Holy Spirit. (More on this in the next chapter.) Jesus is God's Son, and his mission was salvation for mankind.

In biblical times, other descriptive names and titles were sometimes given in addition to a proper name. For example, in Old Testament prophecy the coming Messiah is called "Immanuel" which means "God with us;" one of the titles given to Jesus in the New Testament is "Lord."

CLAIMS ABOUT THE DIVINE IDENTITY OF JESUS

Jesus made bold claims about his divine identity. Many others made the same claims about Jesus.

What claims did Jesus make?

Jesus claimed to be God.

This claim is unique to all other founders of the world's major religions. They may have claimed to be sent by God, to be a prophet or messenger of God, or to be enlightened by God. But, no founder of a major world religion, except Jesus, claimed to be God.

Jesus made the following statements indicating his divine identity.

The Alpha and the Omega

In Revelation 22:13, Jesus said, "I am the Alpha and the Omega, the First and the Last, the Beginning and the End."

I AM

One expression God (the Father) used when identifying himself to Moses was "I AM." In Exodus 3:13-14, we read that Moses asked God, "… Suppose I go to the Israelites and say to them, 'The God of your fathers has sent me to you,' and they ask me, 'What is his name?' Then what shall I tell them?" God said to Moses, "I AM WHO I AM. This is what you are to say to the Israelites: 'I AM has sent me to you.'" When we see these words in the Bible or otherwise, "I am" is normally followed by a descriptive word or words. For example, "I am holy,"

"I am the way." What sets God's "I AM" statement apart in Exodus is the fact that no descriptive word or words followed.

In the following scriptures, Jesus not only made the "I AM" statement referring to himself, but he also declared that he existed before Abraham (who lived many generations prior to Jesus' time on Earth). "'Your father Abraham rejoiced at the thought of seeing my day; he saw it and was glad.' 'You are not yet fifty years old,' they said to him, 'and you have seen Abraham!' 'Very truly I tell you,' Jesus answered, 'before Abraham was born, I am!'" (John 8:56-58).

The next line (John 8:59) confirms that the crowd understood what Jesus was claiming by this statement: "At this, they picked up stones to stone him, but Jesus hid himself, slipping away from the temple grounds." They believed Jesus had committed blasphemy and tried to stone him. Blasphemy could mean one of two things. Either a person said something derogatory *about* God or, as in this case, a person claimed to *be* God. They assumed a person might claim to be sent by God or be a messenger of God, but no man could rightfully make a claim to be God. Blasphemy was punishable by death.

I and the Father are one,

Speaking to a group of opponents, Jesus told them, "I and the Father are one" (John 10:30). His audience considered this statement blasphemy. This is confirmed in their response: "[H]is Jewish opponents picked up stones to stone him, but Jesus said to them, 'I have shown you many good works from the Father. For which of these do you stone me?' 'We are not stoning you for any good work,' they replied, 'but for blasphemy, because you, a mere man, claim to be God.'" (John 10:31–33). As it turned out, Jesus was not stoned because we read in verse 39 that, although they tried to seize him, he escaped their grasp.

Son of Man and Son of God

Jesus frequently referred to himself as the "Son of Man" and sometimes as the "Son of God." The term, "son of man" communicated two different things in biblical times. One meaning was how we would interpret these words today—a man's son. But the people then were also familiar with the following Old Testament prophesy described in Daniel 7:13-14 in which the term "son of man" meant deity: "'In my vision at night I looked, and there before me was one like a son of man, coming with the clouds of heaven. He approached the Ancient of Days and was led into his presence. He was given authority, glory, and sovereign power; all nations and peoples of every language worshipped him. His dominion is an everlasting dominion that will not pass away, and his kingdom is one that will never be destroyed."

When Jesus predicts his crucifixion, he uses this term referring to himself: "As you know, the Passover is two days away—and the Son of Man will be handed over to be crucified" (Matthew 26:2).

In Matthew 16, Jesus asks Simon-Peter in verse 15, "Who do you say I am?" Then we read, "Simon Peter answered, 'You are the Christ, the Son of the living God.' And Jesus answered him, 'Blessed are you, Simon Bar-Jonah! For flesh and blood has not revealed this to you, but my Father who is in heaven" (verses 16-17).

One in essence with God

Jesus often boldly spoke of himself as being one in essence with God:

In John 12:44-45, we read, "Then Jesus cried out, 'Whoever believes in me does not believe in me only, but in the one who sent me. The one who looks at me is seeing the one who sent me."

Jesus told Thomas in John 14:7, "If you really know me, you will know my Father as well. From now on, you do know him and have seen him."

Jesus responds to Phillip in John 14:9: "Jesus answered: 'Don't you know me, Philip, even after I have been among you such a long time? Anyone who has seen me has seen the Father."

The one prophesied about in the Old Testament

Jesus claimed to be the one who Old Testament writers prophesied would one day enter our world—the long-awaited anointed Messiah. (The word "Messiah" is a Hebrew word and when translated into Greek is "Christ.")

In John 4:25-26, we read, "The woman said, 'I know that Messiah' called Christ 'is coming. When he comes, he will explain everything to us.' Then Jesus declared, 'I, the one speaking to you—I am he.'"

Jesus made the following statement just prior to his crucifixion:

> Again, the high priest asked him, "Are you the Messiah, the Son of the Blessed One?" "I am," said Jesus. "And you will see the Son of Man sitting at the right hand of the Mighty One and coming on the clouds of heaven." The high priest tore his clothes. "Why do we need any more witnesses?" he asked. "You have heard the blasphemy. What do you think?" They all condemned him as worthy of death. (Mark 14:61-64)

Metaphors Jesus used to describe himself

The Gate

"I am the gate; whoever enters through me will be saved" (John 10:9).

The Bread of Life

"Then Jesus declared, 'I am the bread of life. Whoever comes to me will never go hungry, and whoever believes in me will never be thirsty" (John 6:35).

The Light of the World

"When Jesus spoke again to the people, he said, 'I am the light of the world. Whoever follows me will never walk in darkness, but will have the light of life" (John 8:12).

The Way, the Truth, the Life

"Jesus answered, 'I am the way and the truth and the life.'" (John 14:6).

The Resurrection and the Life

"Jesus said to her, 'I am the resurrection and the life. The one who believes in me will live; even though they die" (John 11:25).

Quotes from others regarding Jesus

The following are a few quotes about Jesus from Apostles Paul and John:

- "The Son is the image of the invisible God, the firstborn over all creation" (Colossians 1:15).

- "For in Christ all the fullness of the Deity lives in bodily form" (Colossians 2:9).

- "For God, who said, 'Let light shine out of darkness,' made his light shine in our hearts to give us the light of the knowledge of God's glory displayed in the face of Christ" (2 Corinthians 4:6).

- "The Word became flesh and made his dwelling among us. We have seen his glory, the glory of the one and only Son, who came from the Father, full of grace and truth" (John 1:14).

FULFILLMENT OF OLD TESTAMENT PROPHESIES

Jesus was the fulfillment of many Old Testament prophecies.

There are numerous Old Testament verses containing direct predictions about the coming Messiah—his lineage, his birthplace and other prophecies. In addition to these direct prophecies, many interpret other scriptures with subtle depictions of details and events as a foreshadowing of the Messiah. ("Foreshadowing" is defined as "a literary device in which the author gives clues about events that will happen later in the story. Often these clues are fairly subtle so that they can only be noticed or fully understood upon a second reading." [5])

Both of these prophecy types find their greatest fulfillment in Jesus.

Following are a few examples of Old Testament prophecies of the coming Messiah, alongside corresponding New Testament scriptures pointing to Jesus as the fulfillment of these prophecies.

Old Testament Prophecies about the Messiah	Prophecy Reference	Prophecy Fulfilled by Jesus*
He will be a descendant of Jesse's son, King David	Isaiah 11:1-5	Matthew 1:1
He will be born in Bethlehem	Micah 5:2	Matthew 2:1-6
He will be born of a virgin	Isaiah 7:14	Luke 1: 26-38
A messenger will prepare the way for him	Malachi 3:1	Matthew 3:1-3
He will minister to many	Isaiah 61:1-2	Luke 4:17-21
He will speak in parables	Psalm 78:1-2	Matthew 13:3
He will perform miracles	Isaiah 35:4-6	Luke 7:20-23
He will enter Jerusalem riding on a donkey	Zechariah 9:9-10	Mark 11:7-11
He will be betrayed by a friend	Psalm 41:9	Matthew 26:47-50
He will be silent before his accusers	Isaiah 53:7	Matthew 26:62-63
He will be pierced	Zechariah 12:10	Revelation 1:7
He will die for our sins	Isaiah 53:4-9	I Peter 3:18

* Other scriptures may also apply. For the sake of space, only one scripture reference was listed for each prophecy.

Some have suggested that perhaps Jesus intentionally lived out the Old Testament prophecies since he learned them as a child. In other words, he self-fulfilled them. However, Jesus would have had no control over many of these prophecies. For instance, Jesus certainly would have had no control over any of the circumstances surrounding his own birth and early childhood, yet there are numerous prophecies outlining details of everything from his lineage to the place of his birth, the timing of his birth, events that took place when he was an infant, and the town where he was raised. The Old Testament also prophesied other circumstances beyond Jesus' childhood that he could not have controlled.

Others have claimed perhaps the Gospel writers crafted their stories to include prophecies. Sherri Bell addresses this claim in her article, "Only One Person Has Fulfilled All Old Testament Messianic Prophecy. *Jesus!*":

> We have several reasons to believe the Gospel writers reported Jesus' life and words accurately—and did so even at the risk of persecution. They did not play to what their audiences likely expected. We must remember that at the time the Gospels were written, the Christian church was enduring considerable persecution. Many Christians were martyred for their faith in excruciating and inhumane ways, including crucifixion, being burned alive, or being fed to wild animals. The Gospel writers had nothing to gain from inventing yet another new religion—and everything to lose. Too, they didn't make Jesus sound high and mighty, but low and humble, as was His purpose in giving up His life. If the Gospel writers were intent on growing their numbers, they wouldn't have offered up, as Messiah, a man who, in no way, represented the conquering hero that the Jews were expecting. Jesus freely allowed Rome to kill him, so that His purpose was fulfilled.[6]

Is it reasonable to think the Gospel writers would craft, and spread, untrue stories when, by doing so, they would be putting their own lives in jeopardy, risking a gruesome death?

NEW TESTAMENT ACCOUNTS ABOUT JESUS WERE WRITTEN SOON AFTER HIS DEATH.

Contrary to a common misperception, the four biographies of Jesus' life—the Gospels of Matthew, Mark, Luke and John—were not written hundreds of years after his death. If that were the case, it certainly would not render these accounts suspect. But the Gospels

84

were all written soon after Jesus' death. In *Evidence That Demands a Verdict*, Christian apologists Josh McDowell and Dr. Sean McDowell write:

> It can be reasonably argued that all four biographies of Jesus in the New Testament, as well as the book of Acts, were written within a few decades—and certainly within a century—of the events they describe. Even most non-Christian scholars acknowledge this and place the canonical Gospels and Acts securely within the first century. Nevertheless, even if a radically late dating were correct, we would still have records for the events surrounding the origin of Christianity that are earlier than those sometimes used to support unquestioned events in history.[7]

THE NEW TESTAMENT CONTAINS EYEWITNESS ACCOUNTS.

A person reporting an event does not have to be an eyewitness for what they report to be true. In fact, the news reports we read or see on TV are often presented by someone who did not witness the news story. Reporters typically show up at the scene after accidents, crimes, etc. However, it would be advantageous if a reporter is also able to give an eyewitness account. The authors of these New Testament books claim to be eyewitnesses.

> That which was from the beginning, which we have heard, which we have seen with our eyes, which we have looked at and our hands have touched—this we proclaim concerning the Word of life. The life appeared; we have seen it and testify to it… We proclaim to you what we have seen and heard… (I John 1:1-3).

> For we did not follow cleverly devised stories when we
> told you about the coming of our Lord Jesus Christ in
> power, but we were eyewitnesses of his majesty (2
> Peter 1:16).

In addition, the next best thing to a reporter having firsthand knowledge would be for the reporter's source of information to be an eyewitness, or better yet, multiple eyewitnesses. One of the biblical authors, a physician named Luke, tells us that he wrote his accounts based on the testimonies of multiple eyewitnesses. This is how Luke introduces his biography of Jesus in the Gospel of Luke.

> Many have undertaken to draw up an account of the
> things that have been fulfilled among us, just as they
> were handed down to us by those who from the first
> were eyewitnesses and servants of the word. With
> this in mind, since I myself have carefully
> investigated everything from the beginning, I too
> decided to write an orderly account for you, most
> excellent Theophilus, so that you may know the
> certainty of the things you have been taught (Luke
> 1:1-4).

Not only were the books of the New Testament written soon after Jesus' death, but the New Testament's eyewitness accounts once again add to the reliability of the Bible.

THERE ARE MAJOR HOLES IN ALTERNATIVE THEORIES ABOUT JESUS.

The following are three common alternative theories and some of the problems with them.

Theory #1 – The Gospel accounts of Jesus are legends taken from ancient pagan religions and mythologies.

I had been a Christian for many years before I heard about this theory. I explored it further and discovered numerous problems with this claim.

<u>C. S. Lewis responds to the claim that the Gospels are legends in the following quote.</u>

> Now, as a literary historian, I am perfectly convinced that whatever the Gospels are they are not legends. I have read a great deal of legend and I am quite clear that they are not the same sort of thing. They are not artistic enough to be legends. From an imaginative point of view they are clumsy, they don't work up to things properly. Most of the life of Jesus is totally unknown to us, as is the life of anyone else who lived at that time, and no people building up a legend would allow that to be so. Apart from bits of the Platonic dialogues, there is no conversation that I know of in ancient literature like the Fourth Gospel. There is nothing, even in modern literature, until about a hundred years ago when the realistic novel came into existence.[8]

<u>Distortions of myth contents</u>

Some items on lists of "similarities" between the Gospel accounts and mythology distort what is in the myths. J. Warner Wallace, in an article, points out that "it's not unusual for the characteristics of ancient pre-Christian deities to be exaggerated in an effort to make them sound like Jesus."[9] Wallace lists numerous claims from one particular mythology often cited as similarities. He then lists what the myth actually states. When comparing them, it becomes obvious that classifying some of these as similarities is a real stretch. Here are two of the eleven examples he cites.

> Claim: Horus had 12 disciples.
>
> Truth: Horus had only four disciples (called "Heru-Shemsu"), but at some point in his story there is reference to sixteen followers and a group of unnumbered followers who join Horus in battle (called "mesnui").
>
> Claim: Horus was crucified between two thieves, buried for three days in a tomb, and was resurrected.
>
> Truth: Horus is not reported to have died at all in the vast majority of Egyptian narratives. There is also no crucifixion story. Instead, Horus is usually described as eventually merging with Re (the Sun god) after which he "dies" and is "reborn" every day as the sun rises. There is a parallel account describing Horus' death and detailing how he is cast in pieces into the water, later fished out by a crocodile at Isis' request.[10]

Questionable timing

The timing of many of these mystery religions is highly questionable. Josh and Sean McDowell note, "Mystery religions seem to be influenced by Christianity, not the other way around."[11] In support of this statement, Paul Rhodes Eddy and Gregory A. Boyd have this to say.

> A second obstacle to any attempt to understand first-century Christianity in light of ancient Greco-Roman mystery religions is that virtually all of our evidence for these religions comes from the second to fourth centuries … Trying to explain a first-century religious movement by appealing to evidence for a "parallel" phenomenon a century or more later is questionable, to

say the least. True, it is not unreasonable to assume that there were first-century precursors to the mystery cults of the second century and beyond. But this is an argument from silence, and in any case we are left with nothing conclusive about these precursor movements. Hence, any argument that Christianity was influenced by, let alone modeled after, these precursors must be judged as unwarranted speculation grounded in anachronism.[12]

Insufficient time gap

Enough time had not passed between the life of Jesus and the writing of the Gospels for legends to develop. Author Kenneth Boa explains:

[The New Testament] was complete before the end of the first century. There simply was not enough time for myths about Christ to be created and propagated. And the multitudes of eyewitnesses who were alive when the New Testament books began to be circulated would have challenged blatant historical fabrications about the life of Christ. The Bible places great stress on accurate historical details, and this is especially obvious in the Gospel of Luke and the Book of Acts, Luke's two-part masterpiece (see his prologue in Luke 1:1-4).[13]

Syncretism is highly unlikely.

Sean McDowell notes that "Christianity has Jewish roots, not pagan roots." He explains:

First-century Jews loathed syncretism [i.e., the blending of different religions] and refused to blend their religion with others. Jesus was Jewish. And Paul, who wrote several books of the New Testament, had been trained as an orthodox Jew. He held steadfastly to orthodox beliefs about the one true God and would have been unwilling to compromise them for pagan mythology no matter the cost. (See Phil. 3:4-7.)[14]

Differences greater than similarities

Sean McDowell makes another point: "[T]he differences between Christianity and the mystery religions is greater than the similarities." He notes the following example from a myth claimed to be "similar" to the resurrection of Jesus.

> [T]he mother goddess Cybele loved Attis. But Attis was unfaithful to his goddess lover, and in a jealous rage Cybele made him insane. In his insanity he castrated himself and fled into the forest, where he bled to death. Cybele was in overwhelming grief, so she returned Attis "back to life," meaning the body of Attis continued to grow hair and his little finger moved. Is that a resurrecttion?[15]

It is quite a stretch to compare this to Jesus' resurrection.

Similarities between fiction and reality can occur.

Do you have any doubt that a passenger ship named Titanic existed? Do you believe this ship sank and many people drowned in the process? Are you aware of the fictional book, *The Wreck of the Titan: Or Futility* and the similarities between the sinking of the Titanic and the details of this book written by Morgan Robertson in 1898 (14 years *before* the sinking of the Titanic)? Here are some of the interesting comparisons, according to Time Magazine article "Author 'Predicts' Titanic Sinking, 14 Years Earlier" by Heba Hasan.

- <u>Name</u>: In *Futility*, the boat is described as the largest ship of its day and was called Titan.

- <u>Size</u>: The ships were practically the same size, with the Titanic measuring only 25 meters longer.

- <u>Date</u>: Both ships, described as "unsinkable," hit an iceberg and went under in mid-April

- <u>Speed</u>: Both were capable of speeds over 20 knots.

- <u>Safety</u>: Despite having thousands of passengers on board, both ships carried the bare legal minimum number of lifeboats.[16]

Although this fictional story of an ocean liner had much in common with a real event in history, this in no way impacts the fact that the Titanic existed, and that, on April 14, 1912, the events known in history occurred.

<u>History cannot be ignored.</u>

Even if similarities occur between the ancient religions or myths and the Gospels this has no bearing on the fact of Jesus' existence and the well-attested events of his life.

Theory # 2 – Jesus was a great moral teacher, but not God.

In his classic book *Mere Christianity*, C. S. Lewis makes the following comments on this theory:

> I am trying to prevent anyone saying the really foolish thing that people often say about Him: "I'm ready to accept Jesus as a great moral teacher, but I don't accept His claim to be God." That is the one thing we must not say. A man who was merely a man and said the sort of things Jesus said would not be a great moral teacher. He would either be a lunatic on a level with the man who says he is a poached egg or else he would be the

Devil of Hell [lying and misleading others about his identity]. You must make your choice. Either this man was, and is, the Son of God; or else a madman or something worse. You can shut Him up for a fool, you can spit at Him and kill him as a demon; or you can fall at His feet and call Him Lord and God. But let us not come with any patronizing nonsense about His being a great human teacher. He has not left that open to us. He did not intend to.[17]

The life Jesus lived displayed not the life of a liar, not the life of someone who was insane. Jesus' life displayed his true identity—the One worthy to be called Lord.

Theory #3 – The gospel story can't be trusted since some details between the Gospel authors are inconsistent.

Let's first consider some technical explanations for what appear to be inconsistencies in minor details between the four Gospel accounts, and then we will step back and put it all in perspective.

Possible explanations given by Mark L. Strauss

One article reported the following points made by scholar, Mark L. Strauss from an online course he taught, "Four Portraits, One Jesus": "It's important to point out right off the bat that each of the Gospel writers had a particular intention and focus." Strauss says that Matthew is the "most structured," Mark is the "most dramatic," Luke is the "most thematic" and John is the "most theological." Each of them set out to accentuate a specific and unique portrait of Jesus. Through their individual gospels, Matthew, Mark, Luke and John focused on particular elements of Christ's ministry and message that they felt illuminate their narrative. Despite the writers' varied focus, the gospels exhibit a surprising cohesiveness. They all bear witness to Jesus and his ministry but approach the story with an individual perspective."[18]

Strauss' article notes four possible explanations for the apparent contradictions in the gospels and gives an in-depth explanation for each. Following is an abbreviated version:

- Paraphrasing and interpretation – It is a widely held opinion that Jesus' primary language was Aramaic, and he could speak some Hebrew and Greek too. Since the Gospels were all written in Greek, the Gospel authors would have each been translating into Greek whatever Jesus said in Aramaic. Since "translation is interpretation," the different authors could have had minor differences in interpretation.

- Abbreviation and omission – The following example makes this very understandable point: "If you were to ask a husband and wife what they did last Saturday, you're going to get different responses. Maybe the husband will tell you they worked in the yard, went to the hardware store, and went out for lunch. The wife, on the other hand, might tell you, 'We planted rosebushes, talked to our friends Jarrid and Allie (who they ran into at the store), and got into an argument (because the husband ordered a milkshake even though he's lactose intolerant).'... These two stories don't represent discrepancies; they highlight differences in perspective."

- Reordering of events and sayings – "What about Christ's teachings? Was the Sermon on the Mount one long message or did Matthew—like many argue—pull Jesus' various teachings together into one place? From reading Luke, it would be easy to make the argument that the Sermon on the Mount is a compilation of Christ's teaching. But it's just as likely that Jesus taught the same lessons multiple times throughout his ministry."

- Reporting similar events and sayings – "When did Jesus clear the temple? Did it happen once or twice? ... Matthew, Mark, and Luke place this event at the end of Jesus' ministry (Matt. 21:12-13; Mk. 11:15-17; Lk. 19:45-56) but John puts it at the beginning (Jn.

2:13-17). It's not outside the realm of possibility that Jesus felt the need to clear the temple multiple times, but the credibility of the gospels doesn't rest on having to believe that. There's a possibility that Mark moved this event to the end of the gospel to emphasize its significance as an act of judgment against Israel, or that John moved it to the beginning as a historically symbolic inauguration to his ministry."[19]

This article concludes by recommending that should someone find what appears to be a conflict, they first determine whether one of these four issues applies.[20]

Possible explanations given by Michael R. Licona

In Jonathan Peterson's "Why are There Differences in the Gospels?: an Interview with Mike Licona," Licona notes that the writing techniques used by the Gospel authors are consistent with those of other authors in their time. He said those who study classic literature "have for some time recognized [the use of these same writing techniques] in Greco-Roman literature." One example Licona gives is the written works of Plutarch (46AD-120AD), a Greek biographer and essayist. Plutarch reports "the same stories in two or more of the biographies he wrote," and "he told the same stories differently."[21]

One of the writing techniques explained by Licona in this article is called literary spotlighting. According to Licona, spotlighting is "when an author mentions only one person performing an action while being aware of several others who are present." He compares it to a theatrical performance with multiple actors on stage and says, "At one point, the lights go out and a spotlight shines on one of the actors. You know other actors are on the stage. But you can't see them because the spotlight is focused on one person." Licona adds, "Of all the compositional devices I observed being used by Plutarch, literary spotlighting was perhaps the most common."[22]

Following is one example Licona gives where the Gospel writers likely used literary spotlighting.

> In all of the Synoptics [the books of Matthew, Mark and Luke], multiple women visit the tomb and discover it empty, whereas only Mary Magdalene is mentioned in John. It seems likely to me here as well that John is aware of the presence of other women while shining his spotlight on Mary. After all, he reports Mary announcing to Peter and the Beloved Disciple, "They have taken the Lord from the tomb and we don't know where they have laid him" (John 20:2). Who's the "we" to whom Mary refers? Probably the other women who were present. Then observe what happens next. In John, Peter and the Beloved Disciple run to the tomb and discover it empty, whereas Luke 24:12 mentions Peter running to the tomb and no mention is made of the Beloved Disciple. However, just 12 verses later, Luke reports there were more than one who had made the trip to the tomb. These observations strongly suggest Luke and John were employing literary spotlighting in their resurrection narratives.[23]

Literary spotlighting should certainly be considered here and in similar situations.

The big picture

Now, let's step back and consider the big picture regarding this theory.

I am reminded of a scripture where Jesus commented to the scribes and Pharisees in Matthew 23:24, "You blind guides! You strain out a gnat but swallow a camel." In other words, they were so focused on the trivial that they lost sight of the bigger, most important things.

Not all facts and evidence are of equal significance. All should be considered, but some carry more weight than others and deserve greater consideration. This is common in the courtroom setting. Although attorneys may or may not present some of their weaker evidence, they make sure their strongest evidence is presented. Regarding eyewitness accounts, it is more important that the eyewitnesses agree on the major events of their story (the core events). It is less important that they agree on the minor details. In fact, sometimes it can even be cause for suspecting possible collusion when eyewitness accounts are identical on all the minor details.

Even in cases where variances in minor details occur, the law of non-contradiction (as outlined in Chapter One of this book) still applies. Truth exists, even in details. To illustrate, let's consider two witnesses giving statements after a bank robbery. One witness says the robber was wearing a white shirt. The other says the robber's shirt was blue. There is a truth about the color of the robber's shirt. It may have been white, blue, or possibly a pale blue that was mistaken for white. But, no one would say a robbery didn't happen because there is no agreement about the shirt color. In this example, the shirt color is a "gnat." The "camel," the important take-away from these witnesses, is that they agree on the core facts of the story: a man walked into the bank that day with a gun and committed a robbery.

William Lane Craig made this statement when interviewed by Lee Strobel for his book, *The Case for Easter*: "For a philosopher, if something is inconsistent, the law of contradiction says, 'This cannot be true, throw it out!' However, the historian looks at these narratives and says, 'I see some inconsistencies, but I notice something about them: they're all in the secondary details.' "[24]

The bottom line is that the core facts presented in the Gospels about Jesus' death, burial, and resurrection are consistent: Jesus is crucified. Joseph of Arimathea takes his body and puts it in a tomb. A small group of women followers of Jesus visit the tomb early on the

Sunday morning following his crucifixion, and they find the tomb empty. They see a vision of angels saying Jesus has risen.

JESUS PERFORMED MIRACLES WITNESSED BY MANY.

Miracle: An extraordinary and welcome event that is not explicable by natural or scientific laws and is therefore attributed to a divine agency."[25]

I will repeat what I noted about miracles in Chapter 3: "If God has already performed the biggest miracle of all time known to man (i.e., creation), would performing what we call a miracle within that creation be something out of the realm of possibilities for him? In the framework of a worldview in which God exists, miracles are certainly and logically possible."

The Gospels contain reports of Jesus performing about 40 miracles. Even ancient non-Christians reported that Jesus performed unusual feats, but they thought his miracles were some kind of magic. They even referred to him as a sorcerer.

Most of Jesus' miracles were physical healings. Other miracles include turning water into wine (his first recorded miracle), raising the dead, walking on water, calming the storm, and feeding the hungry by supernaturally multiplying food.

<u>Many witnessed the miracles Jesus performed.</u>

Jesus performed miracles in the presence of groups—small groups and sometimes large crowds. The biblical accounts of these events usually mention who was present—the eyewitnesses. Here are two examples:

Jesus said to some disciples of John the Baptist, "Go back and report to John what you have seen and heard: The blind receive sight, the lame walk, those who have leprosy are cleansed, the deaf hear, the dead are raised, and the good news is proclaimed to the poor" (Luke 7:22).

Luke says the following to his audience that witnessed God performing miracles, wonders, and signs through Jesus: "'Fellow Israelites, listen to this: Jesus of Nazareth was a man accredited by God to you by miracles, wonders and signs, which God did among you through him, as you yourselves know" (Acts 2:22).

NOTE: The word "disciples" is used in the recently noted scripture, Luke 7:22, and will be used other times throughout this book, as will the word "apostles." Let's look at the difference between these two words to avoid confusion. Disciple was a term widely used during biblical times and it simply means "student." Therefore, anyone being taught by Jesus, or by John the Baptist, or others was considered their *disciple*. Jesus had many disciples. Jesus' *apostles*, on the other hand, were those he sent out to preach and proclaim his message. People often referred to Jesus' twelve apostles as disciples because they were not only his apostles but also his students (his disciples). *The apostles were also disciples, but not all of Jesus' disciples were apostles—only his chosen twelve.* Sometimes in the Bible when the word disciple is used it is in the broader sense of the word. Other times, it is referring specifically to the twelve apostles. This is an example of how applying context is important for a correct understanding of the Bible.

Why Jesus performed miracles

The Bible gives two main reasons why Jesus performed miracles. Jesus performed miracles to validate his deity, proving that he had authority on earth to forgive sins. We read the following in Matthew 9:1–8.

> Jesus stepped into a boat, crossed over and came to his own town. Some men brought to him a paralyzed man, lying on a mat. When Jesus saw their faith, he said to the man, "Take heart, son; your sins are forgiven." At this, some of the teachers of the law said to themselves, "This fellow is blaspheming!" Knowing their thoughts, Jesus said, "Why do you entertain evil thoughts in your

hearts? Which is easier to say, 'Your sins are forgiven,' or to say, 'Get up and walk?' But I want you to know that the Son of Man has authority on earth to forgive sins." So he said to the paralyzed man, "Get up, take your mat and go home." Then the man got up and went home. When the crowd saw this, they were filled with awe; and they praised God, who had given such authority to man.

Jesus also performed many miracles because he was moved by compassion for the people. This reason is noted numerous times in conjunction with his miracles.

JESUS DIED BY CRUCIFIXION, WAS BURIED, RESURRECTED, AND THEN APPEARED TO MANY.

No one today has probably done more research on the subject of the death, burial and resurrection of Jesus than historian Dr. Gary Habermas. He has committed about four decades of his academic life primarily to the study of historic evidence for the resurrection.

One ongoing study by Dr. Habermas is a review of sources from scholars on the historical circumstances around the death, burial, and resurrection of Jesus to determine what he calls the "minimal facts" scholars agree on. As of 2012, Habermas had reviewed over 3,400 sources published in English, French and German. They include scholars who accept, and scholars who reject, Christianity's teaching about Jesus' deity. Habermas' study is not an attempt to establish views on the deity of Jesus or the miracle of his resurrection, but strictly to determine the areas in which most critical scholars agree on the historical evidence for these events. Habermas reports that "virtually all researchers, whether they are skeptical, liberal, moderate or conservative in their approach and beliefs, agree in recognizing a small but definite core of historical facts from the end of Jesus' life."[26] He notes six of these events on which about 90 percent of the researchers agreed.

1) Jesus died by crucifixion, 2) his early followers had experiences a short time later that they thought were appearances of Jesus, 3) and as a result, they were transformed to the point of being willing to die for this message. Further, two former unbelievers 4) James the brother of Jesus and 5) Saul of Tarsus (later the apostle Paul) both similarly thought that they had seen the risen Jesus, as well; and 6) this Gospel message of the death and resurrection of Jesus Christ began to be taught very soon after these events.[27]

Habermas notes that most of these scholars also agree on more than the above-listed facts, but not at his high 90 percentile standard.[28] Let's look at some of the reasons supporting the authenticity of many of these events.

Jesus' death

Jesus was crucified. This point has overwhelming consensus. Following are just two quotes from ancient *non-Christian* sources specifically referencing Jesus' crucifixion.

> Lucian of Samosata, a second century Greek satirist
> The Christians, you know, worship a man to this day — the distinguished personage who introduced their novel rites, and was crucified on that account… You see, these misguided creatures start with the general conviction that they are immortal for all time, which explains the contempt of death and voluntary self-devotion which are so common among them; and then it was impressed on them by their original lawgiver that they are all brothers, from the moment that they are converted, and deny the gods of Greece, and worship the crucified sage, and live after his laws.[29]

<u>Flavius Josephus, first century historian</u>

At the suggestion of the principal men among us, Pilate condemned him to be crucified…[30]

[Note: Although some words attributed to Josephus are in question as possible late additions, this text is among those widely accepted as authentic.]

It is also widely accepted that Jesus died as a result of the crucifixion. In an article by The Journal of the American Medical Association titled "On the Physical Death of Jesus Christ," the author reached the following conclusion.

Jesus of Nazareth underwent Jewish and Roman trials, was flogged, and was sentenced to death by crucifixion. The scourging produced deep stripelike lacerations and appreciable blood loss, and it probably set the stage for hypovolemic shock as evidenced by the fact that Jesus was too weakened to carry the crossbar (patibulum) to Golgotha. At the site of crucifixion his wrists were nailed to the patibulum, and after the patibulum was lifted onto the upright post, (stipes) his feet were nailed to the stipes. The major pathophysiologic effect of crucifixion was an interference with normal respirations. Accordingly, death resulted primarily from hypovolemic shock and exhaustion asphyxia. Jesus' death was ensured by the thrust of a soldier's spear into his side. Modern medical interpretation of the historical evidence indicates that Jesus was dead when taken down from the cross… Clearly, the weight of historical and medical evidence indicates that Jesus was dead before the wound to his side was inflicted and supports the traditional view that the spear, thrust between his right ribs, probably perforated not only the right lung but also the pericardium and heart and thereby ensured his death... Accordingly, interpretations based on the assumption that Jesus did not die on the cross appear to be at odds with modern medical knowledge.[31]

Peter Kreeft, Christian apologist and renowned professor of philosophy at Boston College, raises these points, among others, in support of Jesus having died on the cross.

Jesus could not have survived crucifixion. Roman procedures were very careful to eliminate that possibility. Roman law even laid the death penalty on any soldier who let a capital prisoner escape in any way, including bungling a crucifixion. It was never done... [And] [t]he fact that the Roman soldier did not break Jesus' legs, as he did to the other two crucified criminals (Jn 19:31-33), means that the soldier was sure Jesus was dead. Breaking the legs hastened the death so that the corpse could be taken down before the Sabbath.[32]

With all the above considerations, it is not surprising that such a high percentage of the Christian and non-Christian sources Habermas' reviewed accept that Jesus died of crucifixion.

Jesus' burial

In his Gospel, John recounts Jesus' burial this way:

Later, Joseph of Arimathea asked Pilate for the body of Jesus. Now Joseph was a disciple of Jesus, but secretly because he feared the Jewish leaders. With Pilate's permission, he came and took the body away. He was accompanied by Nicodemus, the man who earlier had visited Jesus at night. Nicodemus brought a mixture of myrrh and aloes, about seventy-five pounds. Taking

102

Jesus' body, the two of them wrapped it, with the spices, in strips of linen. This was in accordance with Jewish burial customs. At the place where Jesus was crucified, there was a garden, and in the garden a new tomb, in which no one had ever been laid. Because it was the Jewish day of Preparation and since the tomb was nearby, they laid Jesus there (John 19:38-42).

We also learn additional details about Joseph of Arimathea in the other Gospels. The Gospel writers identify him as a "rich man (Matthew 27:57)," "a good and upright man (Luke 23:50)," and "a prominent member of the [Sanhedrin] Council (Mark 15:43)." This Council consisted of the Jewish religious leaders who called for Jesus' crucifixion. Although he was a member of this Council, we learn in Luke 23:51 that Joseph of Arimathea "had not consented to their decision and action."

Another detail we learn through the Gospels is that at least two women who were Jesus' followers witnessed his burial. Author Matt Perman notes the following.

[New Testament] scholars agree that the burial story is one of the best established facts about Jesus. One reason for this is because of the inclusion of Joseph of Arimethea as the one who buried Christ. Joseph was a member of the Jewish Sanhedrein, a sort of Jewish supreme court. People on this ruling class were simply too well known for fictitious stories about them to be pulled off in this way. This would have exposed Christians as frauds.[33]

The Book of Matthew describes the effort made by the chief priests and Pharisees to secure Jesus' tomb:

103

The next day, the one after Preparation Day, the chief priests and the Pharisees went to Pilate. "Sir," they said, "we remember that while he was still alive that deceiver said, 'After three days I will rise again.' So give the order for the tomb to be made secure until the third day. Otherwise, his disciples may come and steal the body and tell the people that he has been raised from the dead. This last deception will be worse than the first." "Take a guard," Pilate answered. "Go make the tomb as secure as you know how." So they went and made the tomb secure by putting a seal on the stone and posting the guard. (Matthew 27:62-66)

Great measures were taken to ensure that the tomb of Jesus was secure.

Jesus' resurrection—the empty tomb

The stone that had sealed his tomb was rolled away the Sunday morning following Jesus' crucifixion: "Suddenly there was a great earthquake! For an angel of the Lord came down from heaven, rolled the stone, and sat on it. His face shone like lightening, and his clothing was as white as snow. The guards shook with fear when they saw him, and they fell into a dead faint" (Matthew 28: 2-4 NLT).

The tomb was empty. Jesus' body was gone.

Had Jesus' body remained in the tomb, the Jewish leaders could have easily put an end to the Christian movement by producing his body to show that Jesus had not resurrected (as Jesus' resurrection was the central message of the Christians).

The earliest Jewish claims about the empty tomb were that Jesus' disciples came while the tomb's guards were sleeping and removed his body. But think about that. To be a Christian at that time was to risk severe persecution, torture, and death. Many disciples were martyred. Why would the disciples risk stealing

Jesus' body and creating a fabricated story about his resurrection when doing so would put them in jeopardy of facing torture and death?

What about the possibility of the Jews or Romans stealing Jesus' body? That would have been senseless. The last thing they wanted was to encourage Christianity to flourish, and an empty tomb would only add to speculation about the Christian's central message—that Jesus had risen from the dead.

Another consideration is that no shrine was set up at the site of Jesus' tomb. Perman says, "This is striking because it was the 1st century custom to set up a shrine at the site of a holy man's bones. There were at least 50 such cites in Jesus' day. Since there was no such shrine for Jesus, it suggests that his bones weren't there."[34]

Even today, we can visit burial sites with the remains of the founders of other major world religions. We cannot visit a burial site containing the remains of Jesus, because over 2,000 years ago his tomb was found empty.

Jesus' resurrection—witnesses

The first Sunday after Jesus' crucifixion, some female disciples (including Mary Magdalene) went to the tomb. Seeing it empty, they initially thought someone had stolen Jesus' body. But an angel appeared to the women and said: "… Do not be afraid, for I know that you are looking for Jesus, who was crucified. He is not here; he has risen, just as he said" (Matthew 28:5). Then the angel instructed them to tell the disciples that Jesus had risen and that they would see him in Galilee.

Soon after the resurrection, Jesus first appeared to Mary Magdalene at the tomb. About a dozen other appearances over a 40-day period were recorded.

J. Warner Wallace comments about the circumstances around Jesus' appearances.

As a detective, I am impressed with cases when they are evidentially diverse. Two witnesses to the same event are better than one. In a similar way, three witnesses are better than two, especially if they agree on their observations in spite of their individual peculiarities or differences. When I have multiple witnesses from diverse ethnic, social, economic or demographic backgrounds and these witnesses generally agree on what they say occurred, I reasonably adopt a higher level of confidence in their testimony. That's why the diverse accounts related to the Resurrection of Jesus are particularly important in assessing the validity of these claims.[35]

Wallace notes that Jesus appeared to different groups at different locations and times. These groups of people were also diverse in terms of the number present and their status in society. He appeared for diverse purposes and periods of time. The authors who recorded his appearances were also diverse.

Wallace concludes that "[T]he expansive and differing aspects of these sightings ought to give us increased confidence in the authenticity and reliability of the accounts."[36]

Peter Kreeft and Ronald Tacelli have this to say in response to claims that Jesus was not fully dead after the crucifixion.

The post-resurrection appearances convinced the disciples, even "doubting Thomas," that Jesus was gloriously alive (Jn 20:19-29). It is psychologically impossible for the disciples to have been so transformed and confident if Jesus had merely struggled out of a swoon, badly in need of a doctor. A half-dead, staggering sick man who has just had a narrow escape is not worshipped fearlessly as divine lord and conqueror of death.[37]

Another point worth noting is that if the authors of the Gospels were making up these Gospel accounts, one would have to question the likelihood of them claiming that women were the first eyewitnesses of the risen Jesus. In that time and culture, the testimony of a woman was barely considered. If their aim was to grow Christianity, this would not have been a good strategy. It would have hurt their case, not helped it.

Also, let's not forget the Old Testament prophecies that mirrored the Messiah's death, burial, and resurrection and were fulfilled though Jesus.

The early impact of Jesus' resurrection

Directly following Jesus' crucifixion, many of his disciples were discouraged and lost hope. They were afraid. They fled and hid. However, days later they encountered the risen Jesus. They were transformed from doubters to believers, from fearful to courageous proclaimers of the resurrected Jesus. The disciples of Jesus were emboldened. Paul and James, the brother of Jesus, claimed to have seen the risen Jesus, and that experience transformed them from non-believers to passionate followers of Christ.

The apostles not only proclaimed the risen Jesus, but they were also willing to die rather than recant what they had witnessed. Some of them were ultimately martyred. According to Sean McDowell, author of the book *The Fate of the Apostles*, there is very strong evidence that four of the apostles died as martyrs: Peter, Paul, James-son of Zebedee, and James-brother of Jesus. As for the apostles Andrew and Thomas, McDowell says there is "good reason to think that they may have died as martyrs as well." With regard to the other apostles, there is not as much definitive evidence about the cause of their deaths. McDowell notes, "[T]he key is not to show that [the apostles] actually all died as martyrs. The key is to show their willingness to die as martyrs." McDowell says their willingness is established in the book of Acts: "The apostles start preaching and proclaiming the risen Jesus. They're threatened. They're beaten. They're thrown in prison... They really believe Jesus had risen from the grave and they were willing to suffer and die for it."[38]

One might wonder how this is different from martyrs today. In their book, *The Case for the Resurrection of Jesus*, Gary Habermas and Michael Licona answer this question.

> [T]here is an important difference between the apostle martyrs and those who die for their beliefs today. Modern martyrs act solely out of their trust in beliefs that others have taught them. The apostles died for holding to their own testimony that they had personally seen the risen Jesus. Contemporary martyrs die for what they believe to be true. The disciples of Jesus died for what they knew to be either true or false.[39]

In addition to the apostles who were martyred, scores of early Christians were also martyred. Tacitus was a Roman historian in the first century. Describing the torture and murder Christians endured at the hands of Nero, he wrote:

> Mockery of every sort was added to their deaths. Covered with the skins of beasts, they were torn by dogs and perished, or were nailed to crosses, or were doomed to the flames and burnt, to serve as a nightly illumination, when daylight had expired. Nero offered his gardens for the spectacle.[40]

McDowell poses this question: "What else could ancient witnesses have done to convince us of the sincerity of their beliefs?"[41]

What is this message that the early church preached and was willing to die for? Paul, a former persecutor of Christians until he encountered the risen Jesus, answered the question this way:

> ... that Christ died for our sins according to the Scriptures, that he was buried, that he was raised on the third day according to the Scriptures, and that he appeared to Cephas, and then to the Twelve. After that, he appeared to more than five hundred of the brothers and sisters at the same time, most of whom are still living, though some have fallen asleep. Then he appeared to James, then to all the apostles, and last of all he appeared to me also ... For I am the least of the apostles and do not even deserve to be called an apostle, because I persecuted the church of God. But by the grace of God I am what I am, and his grace to me was not without effect. No, I worked harder than all of them—yet not I, but the grace of God that was with me. Whether, then, it is I or they, this is what we preach (1 Corinthians 15:3-11).

Christianity grew. The early church established Sunday as the primary day of worship. Followers of Jesus continued the two ordinances he began—the Lord's Supper and baptism.

Jesus impacted the lives of those in the first century and his impact continues today in the lives of men and women, boys and girls.

Truly, "all the armies that ever marched, and all the navies that ever were built, and all the parliaments that ever sat, all the kings that ever reigned, put together have not affected the life of man upon earth as powerfully as that One Solitary Life."[42]

Jesus has been called the centerpiece of the human race for good reason. He is who he claimed to be. He is who his disciples knew him to be. A little over 2,000 years ago, God the Son stepped into our world and carried out his mission—to seek and save the lost.

He entered our world… and he wants to enter our hearts.

ENCOUNTERING GOD

ENCOUNTERING GOD

"The secret things belong to the LORD our God, but the things revealed belong to us and to our children forever." (Deuteronomy 29:29)

"Call to me and I will answer you, and will tell you great and hidden things that you have not known." (Jeremiah 33:3 ESV)

As Jon Morrison states, "Communication through revelation is part of what makes Christianity unique. It takes you from a vague idea of 'there is some kind of something up there,' to a personal God who communicates with us, revealing what he is like and how to have a relationship with him."[1]

Encountering God, we discover what he is like, who we are, why we exist, and how we can live the life for which we were created. He communicates in general ways to all humanity (known as general revelation) and specific ways to specific people (known as special revelation).

We see God's general revelation through nature. In the same way that artwork can communicate things about an artist, we all understand certain things about God through his creation. Romans 1:20 tells us, "For since the creation of the world God's invisible qualities—his eternal power and divine nature—have been clearly seen, being understood from what has been made." We look around at creation, we look up at creation, and deep down we know. We know we are not the master of this universe. We sense there is something or someone greater than us even if we do not attribute what is "clearly seen" as originating from God. We have all encountered God in this general sense.

We also learn about God through special revelation like the Bible, which is our foremost source of information about God.

God is especially revealed to us through the life of Jesus since, as stated in Hebrews 1:3, "The Son is the radiance of God's glory and the exact representation of his being." Therefore, to learn about God, a great place to begin is to read the Bible's New Testament, which centers on the life of Jesus and his teachings.

God can also *speak* to us in other ways, such as through our thoughts (during prayer or any other time), in our dreams or visions, through the written or spoken words of believers, and through events and circumstances. However, it is important to note that any authentic thoughts and impressions of God we have from means other than the Bible will never conflict with the Bible, as the Bible is our primary and unequaled source of revealed truth.

Finally, to whom does God reveal himself? To the open and willing heart of any person who genuinely wants to know him. "You will seek me and find me when you seek me with all your heart" (Jeremiah 29:13).

In the following chapters we will look at some revelations from God: what he is like, what he has revealed about mankind, and our relationship with him.

WHAT GOD IS LIKE

"'I am the Alpha and the Omega,' says the Lord God, 'who is, and who was, and who is to come, the Almighty.'" (Revelation 1:8)

You may have seen some of the artistic depictions of God that I've seen. You know, the very old man with the long white hair and beard, dressed in a glowing robe and sitting on a throne suspended in the clouds. Some may picture God this way. Others might imagine him as the divine disciplinarian in the sky, peering down at us, waiting for us to do something wrong so he can punish us. Maybe we think of God as a cosmic genie we call on when we want something.

Other people may be inclined to see God only in the context of the customs and practices in biblical times. Since their way of life several thousand years ago is so foreign to us in this 21st century, we can mistakenly attribute these same characteristics to God: ancient, obsolete, and irrelevant in today's world.

Maybe we subconsciously view "Father" God through the traits we associate with our earthly father. In psychology, this is known as "transference." This can be good if we have (or had) a father with godly traits but not so helpful to us if our father was absent or if he wasn't a good father. In that case, our impression of fathers may be tainted. Since this usually happens on the subconscious level, we might not even realize our opinion of our earthly father has influenced how we view and relate to God.

Some take liberties to make up their own version of God. This approach is not surprising since many people in our culture think in relativistic terms, believing they can create their own truths. But we cannot re-define God. God is who he is. He created and defined us—not the reverse.

The bottom line is that we can believe God is (or is not) whatever we imagine him to be, but wrong perceptions in no way alter the truth about him.

So, what *is* God like? Let's look at some of what God has revealed to us through the Bible.

REVELATIONS ABOUT GOD

What can we know about God? In short, God chose to reveal to us all we need to know for our present life on earth.

We may not know everything we would like to know about God. Some things about him will remain a mystery for now. Theologian J. I. Packer reminds us, "A God whom we could understand exhaustively, and whose revelation of Himself confronted us with no mysteries whatsoever, would be a God in man's image, and therefore an imaginary God, not the God of the Bible at all."[1] However, we also learn from I Corinthians 13:12 that we will eventually understand what we now consider mysteries: "For now we see only a reflection as in a mirror; then we shall see face to face. Now I know in part; then I shall know fully, even as I am fully known."

Following are revelations about God from the Bible. This list is in no way exhaustive, but I have included some of the most known and discussed descriptions and attributes of God. I also touched on some of this information in previous chapters, and some of what I covered here I will explain in more detail in the chapters to come.

God created our universe—he pre-existed it and he exists independent of it.

"In the beginning God created the heavens and the earth." (Genesis 1:1)

"But do not forget this one thing, dear friends: With the Lord a day is like a thousand years, and a thousand years are like a day." (2 Peter 3:8)

"For in him all things were created: things in heaven and on earth, visible and invisible, whether thrones or powers or rulers or authorities; all things

have been created through him and for him. He is before all things, and in him all things hold together." (Colossians 1:16-17)

We learn in the Book of Genesis (as well as from scientists) that our universe is not eternal, that it came into being at some point in time. Genesis also answers the "who" question: "Who created the universe?" God caused it to come into existence. Since God created the universe, he necessarily would have pre-existed it and therefore, he is independent of it, not subject to what makes up our universe (i.e. space, time and matter).

God is sovereign and the author of truth.

"The LORD has established his throne in heaven, and his kingdom rules over all." (Psalm 103:19)

"The people were amazed at his teaching, because he taught them as one who had authority." (Mark 1: 22)

Jesus said: "Everyone on the side of truth listens to me.'" (John 18:37)

God is sovereign over the universe. Like an artist who starts with a blank canvas and decides what will be, God decided every minute detail of this universe. All truths within our universe, from how things look to how things are and how things function, are based on decisions that originated from the mind of God.

God is more powerful than we can imagine.

"Great is our Lord, and abundant in power." (Psalm 147:5)

What kind of power did it take for God to create the universe? A level of power that mankind neither possesses nor can produce—a level of power beyond our ability to grasp.

God has intelligence and knowledge that is incomprehensible to man.

"'As the heavens are higher than the earth, so are my ways higher than your ways and my thoughts than your thoughts." (Isaiah 55:9)

"Oh, the depth of the riches of the wisdom and knowledge of God!"
(Romans 11:33)

"No one can fathom what God has done from beginning to end."
(Ecclesiastes 3:11)

The design and intricacies throughout creation, from the vastness of our universe as evidenced in over two trillion galaxies to some of the smallest components like DNA, reveal an intelligence inconceivable to us.

God is creative.

"How many are your works, LORD! In wisdom you made them all; the earth is full of your creatures." (Psalm 104:24)

We need only to look around at the variety within creation: the flowers and trees, fish in the ocean, animals, and even us humans to realize that God has endless imagination and creativity.

God is spirit.

"'God is spirit, and his worshippers must worship in the Spirit and in truth.'" (John 4:24)

"The Son is the image of the invisible God" (Colossians 1:15)

The previous scriptures tell us that "God is spirit" and that he is "invisible." What does this mean? It means that God is a spirit-being not comprised of flesh and bones. In the words of Jesus, "a spirit does not have flesh and bones" (Luke 24:39 ESV).

Although there are some references in the Bible such as the hand of God, the face of God, etc., these are symbolic. They are a figure of speech known as anthropomorphisms, a type of metaphor which, in this context, means using human characteristics symbolically to describe things about God in terms that are easier for us to understand.

God is Father, Son, and Holy Spirit (the Trinity).

" The LORD our God, the LORD is one." (Deuteronomy 6:4 ESV)

'Therefore go and make disciples of all nations, baptizing them in the name of the Father and of the Son and of the Holy Spirit." (Matthew 28:19)

God, who is one God, is referred to in the Bible in the persons of the "Father," the "Son," and the "Holy Spirit." The Bible reveals to us that God is *one* God existing in these three distinct persons. At the same time, each person is fully God—not three parts of one God or one God appearing in different forms, but three different persons that are each fully God. One scripture referring to the Son affirms, "For in Christ all the fullness of the Deity lives in bodily form." (Colossians 2:9).

The term used to describe the Father, Son, and Holy Spirit existing as one God is "Trinity." This word was coined by an early third-century theologian named Tertullian. Although this word is not in the Bible, the concept it represents is all throughout the Bible.

Norman Geisler and Frank Turek say, "The Trinity is three persons in one divine essence. In other words, there are three persons—Father, Son, and Holy Spirit—who share one divine nature." Regarding the Son (Jesus), they add: "Jesus shares in the one divine nature, but he also has a distinct human nature." They point out that Athanasius, an early church father, said that, when the Son entered our world, this "was not the subtraction of deity; it was the addition of humanity. Indeed, when Jesus was conceived, he did not cease being God. He simply added a human nature."[2] In Philippians 2:6-7, we read these words of Paul about Jesus: "Who, being in very nature God, did not consider equality with God something to be used to his own advantage; rather, he made himself nothing by taking the very nature of a servant, being made in human likeness." Geisler and Turek also make this statement about the relationship between the Father and Son.

> This is analogous to human relationships. For example, an earthly father is equally human with his son, but the

father holds a higher office. Likewise, Jesus and the Father have different offices but are both equally God (John 1:1; 8:58; 10:30). When Jesus added humanity, he voluntarily subordinated himself to the Father and accepted the limitations inherent with humanity (this is exactly what Paul explains in his letter to the Philippians [2:5-11]. But Jesus never lost his divine nature or ceased being God.[3]

Although the Trinity can be explained to some degree, it is not a concept that we can fully understand in our limited capacity. It is widely considered one of the mysteries about God.

God is personal.

What is meant by "personal?" Having and exhibiting the attributes of a person.

The God of the Bible is not an impersonal force or energy or a distant power. Luke Wayne clarifies this distinction in his article "Is God Personal?".

> In many forms of Hinduism (and in a number of other religious movements) "God" is defined as an impersonal essence, force, or source of being from which every-thing else derives. While personal language may occasionally be used to describe it in a strictly metaphorical sense, this "God" is not a distinct, personal creator with his own intentions, plans, actions, or individual consciousness. In contrast, the God of the Bible is inherently and undeniably personal. [4]

We see many personal attributes of God noted in the Bible. Here are some examples given by Wayne:

The idea of the distinct, conscious, volitional, and utterly personal nature of God runs throughout the Bible. God's will (1 Thessalonians 5:18), His plans (Isaiah 25:1), His compassion, goodness and lovingkindness (Isaiah 63:7), His words (Psalm 78:1), His deeds (1 Chronicles 16:8), and His thoughts and purposes (Micah 4:12) are all inherently personal attributes and actions. God is capable of friendship (Job 29:4), love, and fellowship (2 Corinthians 13:14). God enters into covenants (Genesis 15:18), makes promises (Deuteronomy 1:11), and swears oaths (Deuteronomy 7:8). God knows grief (Genesis 6:6), pleasure (Isaiah 42:21), and wrath (Nahum 1:2)... These are not occasional poetic devices. The personal qualities of God come out on virtually every page and across every genre of biblical literature. [Underlines added.][5]

Based on the definition of the word "personal" and what is revealed about God in the Bible, we can easily attribute this quality to God.

God is righteous and holy. He is the perfect standard. He is light.

"The Lord is righteous in all his ways and faithful in all he does." (Psalm 145:17)

"There is no one holy like the LORD!" (I Samuel 2:2)

"God is light; in him there is no darkness at all." (1 John 1:5)

God is righteous and holy. The word righteous means "morally right or justifiable; virtuous." The primary meaning of the word holy is "separate, set apart, unique." Holy can also mean "righteousness and purity." Theologian J. Hampton Keathley, III explains God's holiness as "that perfection in God that totally separates Him from all that is evil and defiling and common." Keathley continues, "As we call gold pure when it is free from any dross or impurities, or a garment clean when free from any spot, so the nature and actions of God are free from any impurity or evil of any kind whatsoever."[6] God's righteousness and holiness uniquely set him apart.

The Bible also tells us that God is light, and in him there is no darkness. In the article, "What does it mean that God is light?" from gotquestions.org we read:

> Light is a common metaphor in the Bible. Proverbs 4:18 symbolizes righteousness as the "morning sun." Philippians 2:15 likens God's children who are "blameless and pure" to shining stars in the sky. Jesus used light as a picture of good works: "… Let your light shine before others, that they may see your good deeds" (Matthew 5:16). Psalm 76:4 says of God, "You are radiant with light."
>
> The fact that God is light sets up a natural contrast with darkness. If light is a metaphor for righteousness and goodness, then darkness signifies evil and sin. First John 1:6 says that "if we claim to have fellowship with him and yet walk in the darkness, we lie and do not live out the truth." Verse 5 says, "God is light; in him there is no darkness at all."… The message is that God is completely, unreservedly, absolutely holy, with no admixture of sin, no taint of iniquity, and no hint of injustice.[7]

God is holy and righteous. He is the standard of perfection, and he sets the standard for us. He is our moral code.

God is love.

"God is love." (I John 4:8)

It is interesting that this verse doesn't say "God loves" or "God is loving" but that God *is* love. It is his essence. All he thinks and does flows from who he is and, therefore, is rooted in his love.

Some religions (particularly, New Age), twist this truth about God, teaching instead that love is God (love = God). This is an error when referring to the God of the Bible. As previously noted, God is neither an impersonal force nor the emotion we call love. While love is a very prevalent attribute of God, love alone does not define God.

What is meant by the word "love" in the preceding verse? The Greek word used here for love has a very specific meaning. Although there is only one English word for love, in ancient Greek there are different words representing various types of love. Some of these words include *philia* (friendship love), *eros* (romantic love), and *storge* (the kind of love between family members). Another type of love is represented in the Greek word *agape*. Agape love describes a love that is pure and sacrificial and wants the highest good for others. This is the purest form of love. The word agape is used over 100 times in the New Testament. It is the same word used in I John 4:8, describing God. Agape love is the very nature and essence of God, and it is the type of love he has for us, his creation.

God is just.

"He is the Rock, his words are perfect, and all his ways are just. A faithful God who does no wrong, upright and just is he." (Deuteronomy 32:4)

"Righteousness and justice are the foundation of your throne"
(Psalm 89:14)

The word "just" can be defined as "[b]ased on or behaving according to what is morally right and fair."[8] The Bible says all of God's ways are just. All his ways are right and fair—even when he carries out discipline.

God's righteousness and justice go hand in hand. J. Hampton Keathley, III states, "In righteousness we have the manifestation of God's love of holiness, of what is right and good. In justice, we have the manifestation of God's hatred of sin."[9]

Because God is just, he will carry out justice fairly when he judges. The article, "God is Just" at allaboutgod.org contains the following quote about God as our judge.

Many times in the Bible God is pictured as a judge. The Bible says that He will one day judge the world. Many of us shy away from the thought of God as a judge because the examples of justice that we see on earth are flawed: some judges are corrupt and, even when their intentions are good, they can make mistakes. However, the fact that God is just assures us that when He acts as judge, He will administer justice perfectly. His ability to do this involves other aspects/attributes of His character, including His ability to discern the truth in every situation and see into the hearts and minds of men, His wisdom, His strength, His authority, and His moral character in establishing what is right and wrong.[10]

God is merciful and gracious.

"But you, O LORD, are a God merciful and gracious." (Psalm 86:15 ESV)

Although God is perfectly just, he is also merciful and gracious.

God's mercy and grace have been described as follows: "God shows both mercy and grace, but they are not the same. Mercy withholds a punishment we deserve; grace gives a blessing we don't deserve."[11]

These attributes of God are shown throughout the Bible. We see many illustrations of God's mercy and grace extended to mankind. In the following chapter, we will look at his ultimate display of mercy and grace extended to us through Jesus.

"Happy the soul that has been awed by a view of God's majesty."[12]
(Arthur W. Pink)

GOD'S RELATIONSHIP WITH MANKIND

"When I consider your heavens, the work of your fingers, the moon and the stars, which you have set in place, what is mankind that you are mindful of them, human beings that you care for them?" (Psalm 8:3–4)

Who are we? Why are we here? We have an innate desire to know the answers to these questions. God designed us to have this longing. He also provided us with the answers.

Knowing the truth from God's Word gives us clarity and context for our lives. In Chapter 3 ("Reasons to Believe the Bible is Reliable"), I emphasized the importance of context regarding what we read. We need context to understand the author's true intentions. The same principle of context is equally relevant when it comes to our lives. Jeff Cavins explains our need for context using the "storyline" illustration.

> Our desire and fascination with stories suggest that there is an ultimate story of which we are an integral part, a story to which we are drawn that is bigger than ourselves.
>
> As man's longing for God provides evidence for his existence, so the ultimate story, written by God, is evident by our endless search for a plot in which we can envision ourselves participating that will make sense of our lives.
>
> St. Augustine once said concerning our need for God, that "our heart is restless until it rests in you." We could also say that no story will leave us with a sense of completeness and belonging until we enter God's

story. For his story provides the comprehensive story-line by which every life finally makes sense.[1]

What is God's "storyline" for us—the actual context in which we exist? Who are we, and what is the meaning and purpose of our life? What is our problem? In other words, what is preventing us from living out our purpose? Finally, what is God's plan to address our problem so we can live the life we were meant to live? Let's look at what God has revealed to us in answer to these questions.

WHO ARE WE?

The importance of understanding the truth about our identity cannot be overstated, since how we perceive ourselves will greatly influence our lives—for our good or to our detriment.

Who does God say we are as members of the human race? We will examine how the Bible responds to this question. Before we do, here are a few examples highlighting the importance of what we believe about our identity and how our beliefs can impact our lives.

Let's first consider how humanity is defined by two people with worldviews that exclude God. Francis Crick ("agnostic with a strong inclination toward atheism," according to Wikipedia) says, "'You,' your joys and your sorrows, your memories and your ambitions, your sense of personal identity and free will, are in fact no more than the behaviour of a vast assembly of nerve cells and their associated molecules."[2] Atheist Richard Dawkins says, "There is at bottom no design, no purpose, no evil, no good, nothing but pointless indifference... We are machines for propagating DNA."[3]

Imagine looking into the eyes of your child and explaining that this is who he or she is—nothing but "a machine for propagating DNA"; "no more than the behavior of a vast assembly of nerve cells and molecules"; and that their life is "pointless." How would that impact your child's self-image, sense of worth, and purpose?

Of course, it is unlikely that any parent would make this declaration to their child, but if they were honestly representing a godless worldview this is the explanation that applies. As Christian author Natasha Crain points out, if God does not exist, all of creation is here by chance and "[i]n such a case, human life is no more valuable than dust, and there is no basis for saying that any life matters. Only if there is an author of life who creates and imbues us with a meaning greater than our physical parts can lives actually matter."[4]

Regarding the previous examples, I'm not suggesting we avoid these worldviews just because they paint such a bleak picture of humanity. If the evidence was in favor of these assertions (that humans are nothing more than their physical parts), then we would just need to accept that. However, based on the evidence, I think there is good reason to agree with Dr. Francis S. Collins (the scientist mentioned in Chapter 2 who headed up the Genome Project) in his conclusion that the atheist worldview is the "least defensible"[5] and that evidence points to the existence of God.

Here's another example of how what we believe about our identity matters:

I have worked in domestic violence for over 20 years. I once attended a work-related event. One of the speakers was a woman who, in the recent past, had experienced domestic violence, but she was now trying to move on and rebuild her life. She opened her talk by demanding, "Do NOT call me a victim! I am a survivor!" She went on to speak about the importance of being careful about how we frame our life experiences and what labels we accept about ourselves. She understood that seeing herself now as a victim would not help her—but it would hinder her ability to move forward in life.

Intended or not, we internalize what we accept about ourselves, and our beliefs will impact our lives. Our core beliefs matter more than we may realize. We can trust our Creator for the truth about who we are.

What the Bible tells us about our identity

"We are the clay, you are our potter, we are all the work of your hand." (Isaiah 64:8)

"So God created mankind in his own image, in the image of God he created them; male and female he created them." (Genesis 1:27)

"For you created my inmost being; you knit me together in my mother's womb... My frame was not hidden from you when I was made in the secret place, when I was woven together in the depths of the earth. Your eyes saw my unformed body; all the days ordained for me were written in your book before one of them came to be." (Psalm 139:13–16)

Who are we? We are God's beloved creation, created "in his own image."

Although God made many creatures to live on the earth, human beings are unique. Only humans were made in his image.

Before explaining what it means to be made in the image of God, I should note what this does not mean. It does not mean we are a god or that we will become a god. God alone is sovereign. Of course, our likeness to God is not a physical likeness since he is not a material being as we are. However, while we are material beings, we are not *merely* material beings, but each of us is a union of body and soul. (Some use the term "spirit" interchangeably with "soul"). Our body cannot live without our soul, but our soul can exist without our body.

We are in God's image in the sense that we share many of his attributes. We are like God in the following ways: we are personal beings with a mind and a will; we have a moral awareness; we are relational, rational, and in the same way that we see God's creativity throughout the universe, Pastor John Frady notes that we, "often have a built in desire to create things, whether artistic works of art, music, literature, etc., or systems and processes of life."[6]

As God's beloved creation, we have intrinsic worth. This is true of every human being God has created. Our stage of life, physical and cognitive abilities, ethnicity, financial status, appearance, level of education, profession and position in life are not a factor in our worth as persons. Whether we've made mostly good choices or really messed up also doesn't matter. We have worth whether or not we believe we do. *Every* person is valuable to God.

God not only values us, but he also loves us.

It may be difficult to understand how the eternal God who is sovereign over this universe, as massive as it is, even knows who we are, much less, loves us. After all, earlier (in Chapter 1) we looked at the fact that in addition to there being billions of us on Planet Earth, we humans are microscopically small compared to the universe. We could easily walk away from this information feeling quite insignificant and invisible, except for what we know about God. You see, when we compare ourselves to the universe, it is (to us) staggering! But here is where context comes into play. Think about it. What do we know about God that changes everything? We know that God exists beyond space, time and matter. Since God is not subject to space, our size (i.e., the "space" we inhabit) in relation to the massive space the universe inhabits is totally irrelevant to God. It may be mind-blowing to us humans, but this contrast in size is of no significance whatsoever to God.

Although God exists in a dimension beyond our world, he is also present and involved *in* our world. God is personally interested in us and every detail of our lives because we matter to him.

It has been rightly said, "You will never look into the eyes of someone God does not love."[7] Author Jerry Bridges says God's love for us is "affirmed over and over in the Scriptures. It is true whether we believe it or not. Our doubts do not destroy God's love, nor does our faith create it. It originates in the very nature of God, who is love."[8]

WHY ARE WE HERE?

> *"You make known to me the path of life; in your presence there is fullness of joy."* (Psalm 16:11 ESV)

> *"Nothing matters more than knowing God's purposes for your life, and nothing can compensate for not knowing them — not success, wealth, fame, or pleasure. Without a purpose, life is motion without meaning, activity without direction, and events without reason."* [9] (Pastor Rick Warren)

I was 31 years old when I gave birth to my only child, Amy. When I held her for the first time, I remember feeling overwhelmed by the love I felt for her. Although there were other people I dearly loved, parental love was a different type of love than I had ever experienced. There just was (and is) something special about the love I have for my daughter.

Amy recently got married. Her wedding day was an event I had dreamed about from the time she was born. Mothers do that! We look at that little baby in our arms as we're rocking her to sleep and we think about how much we love her. We envision her future and all the special times ahead. There are so many good things at every stage of their lives that we as parents desire for our children. We dream, and we hope, and we pray.

Likewise, God, who brought humanity into existence and who loves us with a perfect love, imagines our future and our potential — who we can become and what we can accomplish in this life with him.

What has God revealed about why we are here? What did he have in mind when he envisioned our lives and our purpose?

First, God created us for himself because he wanted us.

"All things have been created through him and for him." (Colossians 1:16)

"You are worthy, our Lord and God, to receive glory and honor and power, for you created all things, and by your will they were created and have their being." (Revelations 4:11)

We were not only created by God, but we were also created *for* God. As C. S. Lewis said, "Man is not the centre. God does not exist for the sake of man. Man does not exist for his own sake."[10] We exist for God.

Although there is nothing in this universe that God needs (as he existed before the universe began), he willed humanity into existence. God didn't need mankind to exist, but he wanted us to exist — and he wanted *you* to exist.

It has been said that perhaps one reason God created us is to love us. He "takes delight in his people" (Psalm 149:4). We can relate to this in the same way that we delight in loving our children. God takes pleasure in loving us.

We are here to love God and to love others.

"Love the Lord your God with all your heart and with all your soul and with all your mind and with all your strength." (Mark 12:30) Jesus called this the *"first and greatest commandment."* (Matthew 22:38)

"And the second [commandment] *is like it: 'Love your neighbor as yourself.' All the Law and the Prophets hang on these two commandments."* (Matthew 22: 39-40)

What is our purpose? When we hear this question, we might initially think of the very specific assignments we are given to fulfill during our lifetime—such as parenting, our profession, ministry, area of service, or a talent God has given us. In Chapter 8, I will cover more on this. But while our life's purpose will certainly include areas in which we are individually called to serve (that's part of it), the primary reason we exist is greater than the activities we do and the outward things we accomplish. It's deeper than that.

God is a relational being, and so are we. We were created with the desire for relationship and the capacity to love. We long to be loved and to express love. As Christian apologist Abdu Murray says, "We are made for relationships; our desire for fulfilling relationships is universal. That desire in us is explained by looking to our Designer, who is a relational Being."[11] The primary purpose for our existence is to be in a loving relationship with God, our Creator—to love him with all our heart, soul, mind, and strength. This is his desire. It is what he had in mind when he created us. In this context, we also best function, are our best selves, and find our greatest satisfaction.

The second purpose for our existence, which is actually connected to our love for God, is to love others as we love ourselves. If we love God as he desires, that love will overflow to others. These two commandments are so foundational that all of the other laws God has given us stem from these two. In Matthew 22:40, Jesus says, "All the Law and the Prophets hang on these two commandments."

First Corinthians 10:31 tells us, "[W]hatever you do, do it all for the glory of God." If we love God and others the way God instructs us, all we think, feel, say, and do would be emanating from pure love, and this would glorify God. It is not only his desire that we love this way, but these are also commands. Commands reflect not just God's hopes but his expectations.

OUR PROBLEM

We don't always love God and others as we should.

We are commanded to love God with all our heart, soul, mind and strength and to love others as we love ourselves. But even if we try, we know we don't always love perfectly in our thoughts, motives, words and deeds. I don't. You don't. No one does. We all have room for improvement. We can all love better than we do.

All of God's laws are rooted in love. Whenever we do what is contrary to God's laws it is called sin. Sin is often defined as missing the mark. God's perfect love and righteousness is his standard, but we miss that mark. Romans 3:23 confirms, "For all have sinned and fall short of the glory of God."

Because of our sinful nature (our natural inclination to sin) and because sin is so prevalent in our world, we have all become desensitized to sin to varying degrees. We might even be nonchalant about sin, denying the harm it causes. But God takes sin very seriously. He sees it for what it is. It is the root cause of all that is bad and wrong in us, in our relationships, and in our world. Just like we hate cancer (knowing the damage and death it can cause), God is repelled by sin. Because God loves us and has our well-being at heart, he hates sin with a passion.

We are responsible for our sins because we have a free will.

God made his laws known to us, both in his written revelations to us, as well as through the moral code he has "written" on our minds and hearts (Hebrews 10:16). He also endowed us with the gift of free will. Because we have the knowledge of right and wrong and we have free will, we are responsible for our choices.

Right now, you may be wondering, "Why didn't God create us to automatically love perfectly?" Think about that for a moment. Why would that not be possible? Because love always requires freedom. Can you make someone love you? Of course not! Love cannot be forced. It must be chosen. We might be able to force someone to comply with laws and rules, but we can't make them love us. We also cannot make a person *want* to do what is right and loving.

I remember a time when I was a child and had done something that prompted my mother to demand I apologize to my brother. In the most sarcastic and least sincere way, I told my brother, "I'm SORRY!" Then my mother reprimanded me: "Say it like you mean it!" she said. She made me repeat those words several times until they had the sound of sincerity, but my heart was far from sincere. Love is a heart decision that can only be made with a free will.

One more note about free will: free will can only exist if we are presented with at least two options. A person cannot *choose* to love if they are only presented with one option (the option to love). To be able to choose love, we must also have the option *not* to love (to be unloving). We have the capacity to love only because God gave us a free will that allows us to choose—either to love or not to love.

As pointed out by J. Warner Wallace, "Free agency is a dangerous but necessary precursor to love... A world in which love is possible would be a dangerous place. Love requires freedom."[12] This same principle applies to good and evil. Good is only good if the option of evil exists. Therefore, if we want a world in which love and goodness are possible, then the possibility of hate and evil must exist. Otherwise, without options and the ability to make choices, we would be mere robots. By God giving us the gift of free will and options, we have the ability to choose love. As C. S. Lewis noted, "[F]ree will, though it makes evil possible, is also the only thing that makes possible any love or goodness or joy worth living."[13]

Our choices have consequences.

"We are free to choose, but we are not free from the consequences of our choices." (Author Unknown)

Good choices yield good consequences. Bad choices yield bad consequences. The consequences of our choices (good or bad) not only impact our lives, but they can also impact the lives of others—just as we can be impacted by the choices others make.

By choosing well, we have the ability not just to enhance our own lives. We can also make a difference in the lives of others.

What about when we don't choose well? What are the consequences of sin?

The main consequence of sin is that it separates us from God. We read this in Isaiah 59:2: "But your iniquities have separated you from your God." Each sin adds another wedge between us and God. Continual sin so separates us from God that we start losing sight of him. Our hearts become more and more hardened to him and to what is good and right.

Sin also causes destruction and death. Romans 6:23 tells us, "For the wages of sin is death..." Sin sabotages what could have been. When sin entered the world, destruction leading to death followed and created a world that is far from the world we could have had if we had not chosen to sin. Sin damages us spiritually, emotionally, relationally, and physically. We often see direct connections between sin and some of the consequences resulting from sin. For example, someone says something hurtful to a friend, and it evokes an equally hurtful response (damaging the relationship). Someone drinks too much alcohol and does something they regret or gets physically sick afterward. A person does something they know to be wrong and they feel shame and guilt and are robbed of peace.

In God's mercy and grace, he is patient with us, hoping we will turn *away* from sin and *toward* him. But our time is up at some point. One day our body will die, and our soul will depart. Our time to choose differently has passed.

At God's appointed time, there will be a day of judgment, and we will all stand before him. "For he has set a day when he will judge the world with justice" (Acts 17:31). Author Max Lucado makes this observation:

> Judgment Day is an unpopular term. We dislike the image of a great hour of reckoning. Which is ironic. We disdain judgment but we value justice, yet the second is impossible without the first. One can't have justice without judgment. For that reason, "we must all appear before the judgment seat of Christ, so that each of us may receive what is due us for the things we have done while in the body, whether good or bad." (2 Corinthians 5:10)[14]

Our earthly life will be judged against God's perfect standard, and we will all fall short.

What is the final consequence of sin? A place of eternal separation from God. This place is called hell. What is it like? We don't know exactly, but there are metaphors in the Bible depicting it as a place where one exists with the full effects of separation from God—a place void of all that is good, right, just, and loving. If a person chooses separation from God while in the body, that separation from him becomes permanent.

The good news is that this does not have to be our fate. In his love and mercy, God made a way for us.

THE WAY

"Jesus answered, 'I am the way and the truth and the life." (John 14:6)

God provided the way for us to be forgiven of our sins, to be reconciled to him, to walk with him now, and to be with him eternally.

Two thousand years ago God sent Jesus to earth to live among us. He taught us many truths, showed us what a sinless life looks like, and served the needs of many. But his primary purpose for coming was to offer himself as a sacrifice to atone for our sins. He was crucified and died—to pay the penalty for our sins, creating the way for us to be reconciled to God. He carried out this mission willingly. Knowing his crucifixion was soon to come, Jesus made this statement referring to his life: "No one takes it from me, but I lay it down of my own accord. I have authority to lay it down and authority to take it up again" (John 10:18). What prompted him to sacrifice his life for us? Romans 5:8 answers this question: "But God demonstrates his own love for us in this: while we were still sinners, Christ died for us." His sacrifice was a demonstration of his love for us. "Greater love has no one than this: to lay down one's life for one's friends" (John 15:13).

On the third day after his death and burial, God raised Jesus back to life. Many people saw him after his resurrection. They not only witnessed his victory over death, but also witnessed his ascension from the earth about forty days later. This event is the foundation of the Christian faith. Jesus' resurrection confirmed that he was not just another prophet. He is who he claimed to be: God in human form.

Through his finished work on the cross as payment for our sins, and his resurrection which brought victory over sin and death, Jesus made it possible for us to be forgiven, to be reconciled to God, to walk with him here and now, and to be with him eternally.

God made all of this possible for us. How can this possibility become a reality for someone? The following chapter will answer this question.

To reflect on this chapter, let's step back and think about God's relationship with mankind and his willingness to reveal to us answers to some of the deepest questions that we long to understand: What is our origin? Who are we? What is the meaning and purpose of our life? How can we live out our purpose? What happens to us when we die? All these questions were addressed in this chapter.

God—the Author of truth, the source of our existence—did not leave us clueless. Not only did he satisfy the longing we have to know the answers to these questions, but he also stepped down from Heaven to provide the means for us to live the life for which we were created.

A HEART FOR GOD

A HEART FOR GOD

"And may your hearts be fully committed to the LORD our God" (I Kings 8:61)

My daughter and son-in-law recently celebrated their wedding anniversary. I love the saying on a decorative sign they have displayed in their living room. It reads, "You have my whole heart for my whole life."

In the context of marriage, what does it mean to give someone your heart? When a deep and mutual love is present between a man and a woman, it is natural for them to want to commit their hearts to each other in a permanent way. In today's vernacular, this type of commitment means they're "all in!"

Giving one's heart is not just between people in loving relationships. God has declared his love for us throughout the Bible. He even gave the ultimate expression of his love when he sacrificed his life for us, making it possible for us to have a relationship with him.

If you have not already given your heart to God, in the next chapter you will see how this relationship can become a reality for you. In the final chapter, we will explore what it means to walk with God.

YOU ARE INVITED

The Gospel Message

Through his finished work on the cross as payment for our sins, and through his resurrection which brought victory over sin and death, Jesus (God in human form) made it possible for you to be forgiven of your sins and freed from the power of sin, to be reconciled to God, to walk with him here and now, and to be with him eternally.

What must you do to accept God's gracious invitation? Believe, repent, and profess.

Believe

"For God so loved the world that he gave his one and only Son, that whoever believes in him shall not perish but have eternal life." (John 3:16)

This well-known Bible verse has been called the gospel in one sentence. To understand the full meaning of this verse it is necessary to know what the word *believe* means in this passage.

According to *Strong's Concordance,* the Greek word used in this verse for believe is *pisteuo.*[1] Its root word, *pistis,* includes the English definition of believe that we are familiar with: to accept as true. However, this root word has a broader meaning than the English definition. Other meanings given include faith, trust, confidence, and faithfulness.

When you believe in Jesus you accept who he is and the gospel message as truth. You also have and express faith, confidence, and trust in him.

Repent

"Godly sorrow brings repentance that leads to salvation" (2 Corinthians 7:10)

You confess to God that you are a sinner (that you fall short of God's standard of perfect love). You repent by being sorry for your sins. You want to change directions—to turn *from* your sins and *to* Jesus who forgives you, saves you, and shows you the way to true life.

Profess

"If you declare with your mouth, 'Jesus is Lord,' and believe in your heart that God raised him from the dead, you will be saved. For it is with your heart you believe and are justified, and it is with your mouth that you profess your faith and are saved." (Romans 10: 9-10)

What are you to profess? Your faith that "Jesus is Lord." In saying this, you are acknowledging that it is your desire to yield to him, even when his ways conflict with what you would normally think, say, and do. You understand that he, your Creator, knows what is best—what is good and right and just. You are committing to follow him, even when it is not easy.

To whom will you profess this? You will want to let people know about your decision. You will want to acknowledge to others that Jesus is your Lord. But your first profession will be to God in prayer.

Responding to God's invitation

"Give me your heart and let your eyes delight in my ways." (Proverbs 23:26)

Is it your desire to give God your whole heart for your whole life?

If this is what you want

If you believe the gospel message, if you want to be reconciled to God, to turn from your sins and follow Jesus as your Lord, then let God know. You don't need to use fancy words. Prayer is simply talking to him as you would talk to a close friend. You can pray in your own words, or if you prefer, you can pray the following prayer. You just need a sincere heart.

Father God, I believe that Jesus died to pay the penalty for my sins and that you raised him back to life. I'm sorry for my sins, and I'm now turning away from my sins and turning to you. I want Jesus to be the Lord of my life for the rest of my life and I receive him now. Thank you for loving me. I look forward to my new life with you. In Jesus' name I pray. Amen.

If you just prayed to receive Jesus as your Lord, congratulations!

The night I gave my heart to Jesus, soon afterward I had some questions. In case you have questions too, I've included some information for you in the Appendix.

If this is not what you want or you are undecided

People typically give two main reasons for why they decline God's invitation, or delay making a decision—other than simply a matter of the will.

Some have unresolved questions. Although there will always be some unanswered questions in every worldview (as noted in Chapter 1), very often helpful answers to our questions about God, the Bible and Jesus are accessible when we seek them. If you are open to Christianity, but there is a question or questions that stand in your way, I have recommended resources on my website (heartforgod.org) that I hope you will find helpful. Or, you might know someone who has studied the Bible for a long time who can help answer your questions or assist you in researching the answers.

The other reason people often give for their hesitancy in becoming a follower of Christ has more to do with an emotional experience they associate with Christianity than what they believe about Christianity. They may be angry with God about something, or perhaps they had a hurtful experience in a church, or they were turned off by the behavior of someone who claims to be a Christian. If you think a previous experience may be causing your hesitancy toward Christianity, I encourage you to reconsider. Sometimes there are things we can think about God that are not accurate, not biblical. A clergy-member or someone else with biblical knowledge may be able to help clear up possible misperceptions, should that be the case. There are also times when the actions of others who are (or who claim to be) Christians are misrepresenting what Christianity teaches. Remember that no Christian is perfect, and not everyone who claims to be a Christian is actually following Christ. In summary, before you make a decision, make sure you're basing your views about Christianity on what is biblical, not a misperception or misrepresentation of it.

Whatever your reason for hesitating to following Christ, I encourage you to take the time to actively examine what you believe about God, the Bible and Jesus so you can know why you believe what you believe. Seek the truth with all your heart.

If you once committed your life to Christ but at some point you turned back

In the past, you genuinely made a commitment to follow Jesus (perhaps when you were a child), but you have distanced yourself from him. Now you cannot honestly say that in your heart, and in practice, he is the Lord of your life.

God invites you to repent and return to him. As in the parable of the Prodigal Son, your Heavenly Father loves you and eagerly awaits your return. There will be no condemnation when you come home — only a celebration.

The Apostle Paul's prayer for followers of Jesus:

"I pray that out of his glorious riches he may strengthen you with power through his Spirit in your inner being, so that Christ may dwell in your hearts through faith. And I pray that you, being rooted and established in love, may have power, together with all the Lord's holy people to grasp how wide and long and high and deep is the love of Christ, and to know this love that surpasses knowledge — that you may be filled to the measure of all the fullness of God." (Ephesians 3:16–19)

WALKING WITH GOD

"I will walk among you and be your God, and you will be my people."
(Leviticus 26:12)

"The Lord your God is with you wherever you go." (Joshua 1:9)

What a gift it is that we get to walk with God on our life's journey!

When we receive Jesus as our Savior and Lord, we are welcomed into God's family. "Yet to all who did receive [Jesus], to those who believed in his name, he gave the right to become children of God" (John 1:12). As we travel this journey, we do so not with a God who is distant, but with a God who loves us—a God we can call *Father.*

On our life's journey, God is with us every step of the way. He provides what we need. He directs our steps. He also gives us joy for the journey and forevermore.

GOD GIVES US PROVISIONS

"And my God will supply every need of yours according to his riches in glory in Christ Jesus." (Philippians 4:19 ESV)

"His divine power has given us everything we need for a godly life through our knowledge of him who called us by his own glory and goodness."
(2 Peter 1:3)

God blesses his children with many provisions for our journey. Before we look at some of the gifts he has given us, remember that nothing we receive is more precious than Christ himself. No greater gift was ever given. Although God takes joy in giving us many gifts, Christ is and always will be our greatest gift of all.

God gives us a new life in Christ.

"Whoever is united with the Lord is one with him in spirit." (I Corinthians 6:17)

"Therefore, if anyone is in Christ, he is a new creation. The old has passed away; behold the new has come." (2 Corinthians 5:17 ESV)

When we receive Christ, our new life begins!

God gives us the Holy Spirit to live in us.

In John, Chapter 3, Jesus refers to our physical birth as when we were born "of the flesh" but he says we must be "born again"… "of the Spirit." This second birth happens when we receive Jesus as our Savior and Lord.

"[Y]our body becomes the temple of the Holy Spirit, who lives in you and was given to you by God" (I Corinthians 6:19). A temple is a place where God's presence is made known and where people honor God. When you become a believer in Christ, your body becomes a temple in which the Holy Spirit lives, bringing God's presence into your life to change you from the inside. As we seek to live out God's redemptive work in our lives, the Holy Spirit helps us pray (Romans 8:26-27), understand God's Word (John 14:26), gives us awareness about sin and righteousness (John 16:7-11), and produces the "fruit of the Spirit" in us (Galatians 5:22-23).

God gives us a new heart.

We read in Ezekiel 36:26, "I will give you a new heart… I will remove from you your heart of stone and give you a heart of flesh." In this context, a heart of flesh means a tender heart. God softens our hearts and fills them with his love: "God's love has been poured out into our hearts through the Holy Spirit, who has been given to us" (Romans 5:5).

God gives us his written Word.

"Your word is a lamp for my feet, a light on my path." (Psalm 119:105)

The Bible is one of God's greatest gifts to us. It helps us get to know him in a deeper way. We have the privilege of reading it, studying it, and as the Psalmist recommended, storing it up in our hearts (Psalm 119:11).

If you are new to the Bible, where should you begin? As mentioned previously, since Jesus is "the exact representation" of God (Hebrews 1:3) and since God's new covenant is the covenant that applies to us today, the New Testament is a great place to begin reading and studying the Bible. Within the New Testament, many people recommend beginning with the books of John and Romans.

Churches often hold Bible studies for small groups. Everyone can benefit from studying God's Word in this setting, and it is especially helpful to those new to the Bible. If you happened to skip over Chapter 3 of this book, it would be helpful to go back and read it—to learn about the uniqueness and history of the Bible and to understand the importance of reading the Bible in context. Reading the Scriptures in context will help you better understand what the authors were communicating. Without context, misinterpretations will happen. It also helps to have a pastor, or someone else who has studied the Bible for a long time, to go to when questions arise about what you are reading.

God's Word will reveal many truths to us and instruct us in what it means to live in Christ. Jesus said, "I have come that they may have life, and have it to the full" (John 10:10). The Bible is our guide to the "full" life, to the "life that is truly life" that living in Christ brings. God is describing in detail what loving well looks like when he tells us, through his commands and instructions, what to do and what to avoid. His instructions are designed to help us love better—to love him better, to love others better and to love ourselves better. Loving well will give us the most satisfying, enjoyable, peace-filled lives. His instructions are for our good, individually and collectively.

God gives us prayer – a means to communicate with him.

We communicate with God through prayer. Prayer is simply sharing with him from our hearts in words that come naturally to us. Sometimes written prayers can also reflect what is on our hearts. The important thing is that the words we pray mirror what we are thinking and feeling when we talk to God. What do we share with him? Through prayer:

We express acknowledgment of who God is.

"As the heavens are higher than the earth, so are my ways higher than your ways and my thoughts than your thoughts." (Isaiah 55:9)

"Worthy are you, our Lord and God, to receive glory and honor and power, for you created all things, and by your will they existed and were created." (Revelation 4:11 ESV)

When we address God as "Father" or "Lord," we are acknowledging who he is in relation to us. We can also reflect on his attributes that we come to know as we walk with him, such as his sovereignty, love, goodness, and other traits.

We express our gratitude to God.

"It is he who made us, and we are his; we are his people, the sheep of his pasture. Enter his gates with thanksgiving and his courts with praise; give thanks to him and praise his name. For the LORD is good and his love endures forever; his faithfulness continues through all generations." (Psalm 100: 3-5)

We express thanks for God's love for us, what he has done for us, his provisions, gifts, blessings, and anything else for which we are grateful.

We also thank him for the good that has come, or we trust will come through unlikely and even difficult circumstances. "Rejoice always, pray continually, give thanks in all circumstances; for this is God's will for you in Christ Jesus" (I Thessalonians 5:16-18). "And we know that in all things God works for the good of those who love him, who have been called according to his purpose." (Romans 8:28).

We "get real" with God by confessing our feelings and failures.

"Trust in him at all times, you people; pour out your hearts to him, for God is our refuge." (Psalm 62:8)

"If we confess our sins, he is faithful and just and will forgive us our sins and purify us from all unrighteousness." (I John 1:9)

One thing that is clear in the Bible is that God's children openly shared their deepest feelings when they prayed to him. They expressed their true emotions. Our thoughts and feelings are of no surprise to God. After all, he is all-knowing. He knows what we are feeling and thinking, even before we open up to him. It is just beneficial to us and our relationship with God that we acknowledge the truth. We can trust him with our deepest feelings, whatever they are. God is the author of truth. He loves honesty!

We confess to God where we have failed and where we have sinned. We acknowledge whatever it is we did or didn't do that falls short of his perfect love and righteousness. We regret that we chose poorly, and we confess that to God. (I address more about this later in this chapter.)

We ask God for guidance

"But when he, the Spirit of truth, comes, he will guide you into all the truth." (John 16:13)

On our life's journey we will have many choices to make along the way. It is easy to know God's will for some decisions we make because his Word addresses many life topics. But we won't find direct guidance in the Bible for other choices we have to make, such as: which school to attend, what career path to pursue, who we should date or marry, whether to accept the job we've been offered, where to live, etc. We will want to ask God for his guidance.

Additionally, when seeking God's will for a decision, an important question to ask ourselves is whether we are living in obedience to God in what he has already revealed to us. The more we are living in Christ, the better clarity we will have about God's will in all circumstances.

We share with God our hopes and desires.

"Present your requests to God." (Philippians 4:6)

We share our hopes and desires with God. We know without a doubt that he can do anything we ask, as he is the One who created this universe, so he's able to do (within this universe) anything he chooses.

Also, because we understand that God knows more than we do, we let him know that if what we desire is not what is best, we want his perfect will more than our own will. Jesus modeled this for us in the Garden of Gethsemane before he was crucified. He prayed to the Father, "[N]ot my will, but yours be done" (Luke 22:42). Jesus acknowledged that his desire (the desire of his human nature) was to not experience the pain and agony of the crucifixion, yet he yielded to the divine will he shares with the Father. Jesus was willing to be crucified so we could be redeemed.

How does God communicate with us?

We communicate to God through prayer, but how does God communicate to us in response to our prayers?

Sometimes he responds to us while we are praying, through a very clear and distinct thought. He will put a scripture or a message in our mind. Isaiah 30:21 describes it this way: "And your ears shall hear a word behind you, saying, 'This is the way, walk in it.'" This is not an audible voice, but the Bible describes it in I Kings 19:12 as "a gentle whisper." Or, a strong feeling might wash over us—as a "yes" or "no" in response to something we ask him.

God can also respond to us at some point after we pray. His response may come while we are reading the Bible. A verse will give us the answer we are seeking. He can answer us through the written or spoken words of other believers, through events and circumstances, and even possibly through a dream or vision. However, I will repeat what was mentioned in a previous chapter: the Bible is our primary and unequaled source of God's revelation to us so nothing God is communicating to us would ever conflict with the Bible. One of the benefits of studying God's Word is that it helps us to discern if something we think God is communicating to us, is or is not in alignment with what is revealed in the Bible.

God may not always give us the answer to our prayers in the timeframe we would like. This is when we can exercise patience and trust that, if we are walking in Christ, he will respond to our prayers in his timing.

God gives us a family.

"See what great love the Father has lavished on us, that we should be called children of God! And that is what we are!" (1 John 3:1)

"You are members of God's family." (Ephesians 2:19 NLT)

When God became our Father, we also inherited brothers and sisters. We are part of the family of God. We will come together as a family for worship (which also includes the two ordinances established by Jesus: baptism and communion); for fellowship; for teaching and spiritual growth; and to serve together. (I address more on spiritual growth and serving later in this chapter.)

Worship

"Ascribe to the LORD the glory due his name; worship the LORD in the splendor of his holiness." (Psalm 29:2)

"Then will I go to the altar of God, to God, my joy and my delight." (Psalm 43:4)

"Come, let us bow down in worship, let us kneel before the LORD our Maker." (Psalm 95:6)

"Worship the LORD with gladness; come before him with joyful songs." (Psalm 100:2)

One definition of the word worship is "adoring reverence or regard."[1] Worship is first and foremost a belief and attitude. We can worship God any time, with or without other people, no matter where we are. But church allows us to come together with our faith family for corporate worship. In addition to hearing the teaching of God's Word, we participate in outward expressions of what is felt inwardly — such as bowing in prayer, kneeling and singing. When lived out as God intended, worship will not just be religious activities we include in our schedules but what flows naturally through our lives in Christ.

<u>Fellowship</u>

"For where two or three gather in my name, there I am with them."
(Matthew 18:20)

"They devoted themselves to the apostles' teaching and to fellowship, to the breaking of bread and to prayer." (Acts 2:42)

"Therefore, as we have opportunity, let us do good to all people, especially to those who belong to the family of believers." (Galatians 6:10)

One article has this to say about fellowship:

> The Christian life is designed to be enjoyed with others. Jesus invested much of His ministry with 12 disciples as His closest friends. He likewise calls us to live in community with one another. The New Testament has over 50 "one another" verses that refer to loving one another, serving one another, encouraging one another, and praying for one another. Each of these commands requires relationships with other Christians.[2]

Churches often provide opportunities for meaningful fellowship. It is usually in the smaller group settings where we can really get to know each other, grow closer to our brothers and sisters in Christ, and care for each other when personal needs arise.

GOD DIRECTS OUR STEPS

"Follow God's example, therefore, as dearly loved children and walk in the way of love, just as Christ loved us and gave himself up for us."
(Ephesians 5: 1–2)

As we travel on our life's journey, we are told to "walk in the way of love." Jesus is our guide. "He guides me along the right paths for his name's sake" (Psalm 23:3). He leads us to what love was intended to be—perfect love. Jesus tells us, "I am the way" (John 14:6), "follow me" (John 12:26). Along the way, he helps us grow in maturity and love.

Growing in maturity

In the Bible, new Christians are sometimes referred to as "babies." We are told, "Like newborn babies, crave pure spiritual milk, so that by it you may grow up in your salvation" (I Peter 2:2). It was never intended that we would start our journey with the Lord and then stop. God wants us to grow so we become mature. "Let perseverance finish its work so that you may be mature and complete, not lacking anything." (James 1:4)

God wants to work within us to grow us into maturity for our completeness and the benefit of others, so he can love others through us. The work he does within us and through us is referred to as "good works": "we are his workmanship, created in Christ Jesus for good works, which God prepared beforehand, that we should walk in them" (Ephesians 2:10). We are saved *from* the penalty and power of sin, and we are saved *for* good works.

In this context, "good works" has a much broader meaning than we typically think of when we use that phrase. While helping with the community food pantry or teaching a Bible study class can certainly be good works, the good works God wants to do within us and through us encompasses our whole life—all we are and all we do, and it requires our cooperation, as we still have a free will after we accept Christ. The purpose of good works is to glorify God. In I Corinthians 10:31, we read, "[W]hatever you do, do it all for the glory of God."

I should also note this about good works: A person does not earn their salvation by doing good works. That is not how we are reconciled to God. "For by grace you have been saved through faith. And this is not your own doing; it is the gift of God" (Ephesians 2:8 ESV). Our redemption is a *gift* from God—purchased by the finished work of Jesus on the cross as payment for our sins—and the only means to a right relationship with God. It is extended to us "by grace," and we accept it "through faith." Although good works are not the basis for salvation, genuine salvation will result in God's Spirit working to change our hearts. The good works done in our hearts will find expression in and through our lives. "As water reflects the face, so one's life reflects the heart" (Proverbs 27:19).

Tossing the "bad stuff"

"[Jesus] *gave himself for us to redeem us from lawlessness and to purify for himself a people for his own possession who are zealous for good works."* (Titus 2:14 ESV)

God's love in our hearts will change and "purify" us. When our hearts are truly changed, it will begin to impact everything about us—our thoughts, attitudes, words, and behavior. As we walk in Christ, he will (in simplistic terms) decrease the "bad stuff" in us and increase the "good stuff."

For many years I taught seminars on getting organized. I covered several topics, but the organizational system that people were most interested in was "Conquering Clutter." All of this "stuff" in their home they once enjoyed, they now called "clutter." They said the clutter weighed them down. It was a barrier to the life they envisioned. They wanted to be free of their clutter, and now they were ready to "throw out" this stuff that was in their way. They also came to understand that giving up the clutter would lead to wonderful benefits: their home would be more aesthetically pleasing; they would feel more relaxed in it; it would be easier to clean; and they would be more likely to invite company over. They realized that de-cluttering is a process, and the more clutter they got rid of, the more benefits they would be able to enjoy.

So it is with the "stuff" in our lives as we allow God to purify us from the bad stuff—the thoughts, attitudes, words and behaviors that God's Word tells us to avoid. We read in Hebrews 12:1-2, "let us throw off everything that hinders and the sin that so easily entangles. And let us run with perseverance the race marked out for us, fixing our eyes on Jesus, the pioneer and perfecter of faith." The Bible tells us that although sin may bring us "fleeting pleasures" (Hebrews 11:25), it always leads to consequences. It weighs us down. It entangles us. It is a barrier to what our lives can be and what God can do through our lives. Seeing sin for what it is, we will want to throw it off as God has instructed us so we can enjoy the benefits of de-cluttered lives.

Before God changes a heart, it is to varying degrees desensitized or hardened to sin. When we become a child of God we become more aware of our shortcomings because of God's Spirit living in us. Some thoughts, attitudes, words, and behaviors just won't feel right anymore. They conflict with our new God-given desire to love well (to love God well, to love others well, and to love ourselves well). We can also ask God to reveal to us where we fall short. Psalm 139: 23–24 says, "Search me, God, and know my heart; test me and know my anxious thoughts. See if there is any offensive way in me, and lead me in the way everlasting."

Once we are aware of our sin, will we then become sinless? Will we always do what is good and right and just? Will we love perfectly all the time? No. We still have the capacity to sin. We still have a free will, and sometimes we will choose poorly. Regardless of how much we grow, we will not be consistent 100 percent of the time. Even the Apostle Paul, who wrote much of the New Testament, lamented over his inconsistencies. He said, "what I want to do I do not do," and, "I do what I do not want to do" (Romans 7:15-16). God's Word tells us that we will not love perfectly while we are on this earth: "If we claim to be without sin, we deceive ourselves and the truth is not in us" (I John 1:8).

Does that mean we should give up because we won't meet God's perfect standard? Does it mean we can be nonchalant about the sin in our lives? Can we say (when we don't love well), "It is what it is. That's just how I am."? Of course not! We should never be accepting of, or comfortable with any sin in our lives. Now that God's Spirit lives in us and we understand the damage sin does, what it costs us, how it impacts others, and especially what it cost Jesus, we must never become comfortable with our sin. (I Peter 2:24 reminds us, "'He himself bore our sins in his body on the cross, so that we might die to sins and live for righteousness.'") When we do sin, it won't feel right. There will be a discomfort. Just as a signal light on a car's dashboard warns us, the Holy Spirit warns us that something is not right—that we need to avoid something or change something.

What about the temptations and inner struggles we have? And what about when we sin? Knowing that these scenarios would be part of our experiences, our Father gave us the following provisions:

The Bible talks about the inner struggles we will have between the "flesh" (our old nature) and the Spirit: "For the flesh desires what is contrary to the Spirit, and the Spirit what is contrary to the flesh. They are in conflict with each other" (Galatians 5:17). Our flesh may want to think, say or do one thing, but if we know that what we want is counter to God's will and we respond in Christ, we will yield to our Father's will. The longer we live in Christ, not only will we grow in maturity, but our desires will also gradually begin to change to match God's desires. We "are being transformed into his image with ever-increasing glory, which comes from the Lord, who is the Spirit" (2 Corinthians 3:18). "The path of the righteous is like the morning sun, shining ever brighter till the full light of day" (Proverbs 4:18). The more we grow, we will have less and less inner struggle because we will start to *want* what God wants.

What about when we are tempted to sin? Regarding temptation, the Bible tell us, "God is faithful; he will not let you be tempted beyond what you can bear. But when you are tempted, he will also provide a way out so that you can endure it" (I Corinthians 10:13). Also, one of the fruits of the Spirit is self-control. God gives us the ability to resist temptation. If we respond in Christ, we will choose God's way, resisting the temptation.

What about times when we do not choose well? The Bible says, "if anybody does sin, we have an advocate with the Father—Jesus Christ, the Righteous One" (I John 2:1). We must confess our sins, acknowledging our wrongdoing. "If we confess our sins, he is faithful and just and will forgive us our sins and purify us from all unrighteousness" (I John 1:9). Even though we may experience regret and consequences over our sins, we do not have to carry the weight of condemnation. God's Word tells us, "there is now no condemnation for those who are in Christ Jesus" (Romans 8:1). God just wants us to make amends for our sins (when that is possible) and choose differently next time.

Enjoying the "good stuff" – joy for the journey

"Blessed are those who hunger and thirst for righteousness, for they will be filled." (Matthew 5:6)

"We continually ask God to fill you with the knowledge of his will through all the wisdom and understanding that the Spirit gives, so that you may live a life worthy of the Lord and please him in every way: bearing fruit in every good work, growing in the knowledge of God" (Colossians 1:9–10)

"I am the vine; you are the branches. If you remain in me and I in you, you will bear much fruit" (John 15:5)

Jesus referred to himself as the "vine" and we as the "branches," and he said if we remain in him, we will grow and "bear much fruit." Growth is a process. Sometimes there will be growth spurts. Other times growth will be slow. Sometimes we may go three steps forward and two steps back. Remember, God is our loving Father and he is patient with us.

What is the fruit (the "good stuff") that will increase in our lives as we grow in Christ? Below is a partial list from God's Word of his gifts to us. Galatians 5:22-23 calls these gifts that result from life in Christ, the "fruit of the Sprit." As you read this list, imagine your life with these gifts that God wants for you—that are increasingly yours as you mature in Christ.

Love	Goodness
Joyfulness	Faithfulness
Peacefulness	Gentleness
Patience	Self-Control
Kindness	

Growing in love

"Love the Lord your God with all your heart and with all your soul and with all your mind and with all your strength." (Mark 12:30)

"Love your neighbor as yourself" (Mark 12:31)

We often think of love as an emotion. Although we can (and usually do) experience emotions with love, genuine love begins with a decision. Love is a choice. This is good because sometimes we may not feel like loving, but we can still choose to respond lovingly. When Jesus tells us to love one another, the word "love" is used as a verb. It is not just a feeling of love, it is what we do, how we behave and how we respond.

When we are walking with God and living in Christ, we will increasingly grow in maturity, and love. More than an emotional feeling, the love in our hearts will be expressed within us and through us.

<u>Loving God well</u>

Jesus tells us the "first and greatest" commandment is to love God with all our heart, all our soul, all our mind, and all our strength. This means to love God with our whole being and give him first place in our lives.

We can express our love to him in worship and through prayer (which we covered earlier).

We can love God by wanting to (and making the effort to) get to know him better. Just like when we are interested in having a relationship with a person, we will make time for them and take an interest in them. We are intentional about getting to know them. The main ways we get to know God are through prayer and studying his Word.

We express love to God by letting him lead us and doing his will because we *want* to please him. As the Psalmist wrote, "I desire to do your will" (Psalm 40:8).

We exhibit the love we have for God by loving others. As mentioned previously, the two are connected. In the remainder of this section we will look at what it means to love others well.

<u>Loving others – as we love ourselves</u>

We are commanded to love others as we love ourselves. This is not a command to love ourselves. Instead, the command is to love others — and the measure with which we are to love others is *as* we love ourselves. If that is the measure for loving others, then what does *loving ourselves* mean in this context? How should we view ourselves? How should we feel about ourselves?

God is the Author of truth. He wants us to have a correct view of ourselves—to not think more highly or lowly of ourselves than we should. "Do not think of yourself more highly than you ought, but rather think of yourself with sober judgment, in accordance with the faith God has distributed to each of you" (Romans 12:3). To think soberly about ourselves is to base what we think of ourselves and how we feel about ourselves on God's truth. We were created in his image, and although in exercising our free will we have fallen short of his perfect standards, we have intrinsic worth, and we are loved by him.

If we think more highly of ourselves than we should, we become pre-occupied with ourselves. If we think lowly of ourselves, we can also become pre-occupied with ourselves, but in a different way — trying to measure up and obtain the God-given worth we do not acknowledge we have. When we have a correct view of ourselves and see ourselves as God sees us, we will feel complete and whole. We are not pre-occupied with ourselves and thereby freer to love others.

When we accept Christ, we will begin to grow in our acceptance of God's truths, including truths about ourselves. We will begin to grow in loving ourselves as God meant for us to love ourselves as opposed to some of the ways that our culture may encourage us to love ourselves. We will grow in ways that look more like self-acceptance, self-respect, and acknowledgement of who God says we are.

We will also accept others despite their shortcomings in the same way God has accepted us with our shortcomings; we will respect others and love them as we love ourselves.

Loving others in our day-to-day lives

We all have opportunities in our day-to-day lives to express God's love to people, such as tuning in and responding to the needs of our family members, friends, and neighbors; and being helpful at home or work or school. It may be sending someone a note of encouragement; inviting someone over for dinner who would enjoy the company; kindnesses extended to strangers we encounter in the course of our day, and other expressions of love.

Loving others well is simply about being mindful of others and responding to them in ways that flow naturally from a heart full of God's love, treating others the way we would like to be treated and loving them as we love ourselves.

Loving others in tough situations

Often, an expression of love carries with it a "warm, fuzzy" feeling, making it an easy choice. In certain situations, loving others may not be so simple.

For example, when parents have set reasonable boundaries for their child, yet the child disregards the rules, the parents' most loving response will be appropriate discipline. It is not always easy for parents to set and enforce rules because doing so doesn't evoke that "warm, fuzzy" feeling that usually accompanies expressions of love, but it is clearly in the best interest of their child. In fact, failure to discipline one's child is detrimental to that child. Appropriate discipline helps children live peacefully with themselves and in the world and helps them behave in ways that benefit themselves and others. As we read in Hebrews 12:11, "[Discipline] produces a harvest of righteousness and peace for those who have been trained by it." Discipline is what parents do as an expression of the love they have for their child, even though it may not be easy.

Here is one more example of loving others in a tough situation:

How does a person respond in love to someone who has become their enemy? There is quite a range here of what could constitute an enemy. On one end of the spectrum, it may simply be someone with whom they have had a disagreement. On the other end of the spectrum, it could be as serious as someone who has done physical harm to them. (I see this regularly in my work helping those who have experienced domestic violence.)

Regardless of the degree of the offense, Jesus tells us that loving others includes loving our enemies. He tells us to pray for them (Luke 6:28). He also tells us to forgive our enemies. But what does forgiveness mean, especially regarding our enemies?

Forgiveness means releasing any desire to retaliate and letting go of bitterness. It does not mean minimizing or condoning the injustice that has been done, and forgiveness does not always include reconciliation. Although, in many situations, reconciliation can be good and desirable, it is not required for forgiveness, especially in cases where reconciling would not be safe. As Pastor Rick Warren said, "Just because you respond to an offender lovingly doesn't mean you continue to allow injustice."[3] In those circumstances, we can still love our enemies by forgiving them and praying for them. Additionally, a person may have a desire to forgive someone and decide to forgive them soon after an offense. Even so, genuine forgiveness is a process that often takes time. Generally, the more serious the offense, the more time it can take, but it is worth the pursuit. There is no place for unforgiveness (bitterness and retaliation or the desire to retaliate) in the hearts of those who seek to follow Christ. God wants our hearts to be free of that "bad stuff."

<u>Loving others through service and ministry</u>

Jesus "did not come to be served, but to serve." (Matthew 20:28)

Some people have musical talent. A friend of mine volunteers at a hospital, playing her flute in the lobby. Those with the ability to sing well can bring glory to God by inspiring others with their beautiful voice and uplifting lyrics. Someone else may use their gift of teaching to help others. Another person who has leadership qualities can serve in that capacity. Whatever gifts and talents we have can be shared for the benefit of others.

We may have a career that directly ministers to people's needs. Someone may work in the medical field or at a non-profit organization that provides direct assistance to people. Even when our profession does not directly minister to people, our place of employment is still a place of ministry, as we can express God's love to those with whom we work and to others we encounter through the course of our work.

God can also (and often does) call us to help in an area of service or ministry that holds some significance to us personally. Life experiences equip us in a way that allows us to connect at a deeper level with others who share that same experience. For instance, someone who has gone through cancer may volunteer at a hospital helping cancer patients. Someone who overcame poverty might be able to teach those who are struggling financially how to budget and how to gain financial independence.

There are many churches and organizations that provide opportunities to serve and minister to others with the time, energy, and resources God has given us. We can ask God to help us identify a place for us to serve that fits with our specific gifts or talents, or areas of interest. Until we are clear on what area of service is the right fit for us, we can let the needs around us determine where we serve. Even when we are serving in the area of our calling, we can still be sensitive to the needs around us and help when we can.

Loving others by sharing the Good News with them

"For I am not ashamed of the gospel, because it is the power of God that brings salvation to everyone who believes." (Romans 1:16)

"Let the redeemed of the Lord tell their story." (Psalm 107:2)

"I consider my life worth nothing to me; my only aim is to finish the race and complete the task the Lord Jesus has given me—the task of testifying to the good news of God's grace." (Acts 20:24)

There is something I've always done that my mother didn't like. Whenever someone compliments me on a dress or outfit I'm wearing, if I bought it at a really good sale price, I love letting them know what I paid for it and where they can buy it. My mom would scold me and tell me I shouldn't announce it. But I knew how much joy I had in buying that outfit, and I wanted others to be able to have the same joy. How could I not share it with them?

There are so many in our world who need to hear the gospel. Those of us who are in Christ have the opportunity to tell them that God can do for them what he has done in our lives. We don't have to wait to share the Good News till we're perfect. We will never be. We don't have to wait till we have all the answers. We will never have all the answers. We just need a willing heart that cares about others and wants them to come to know the Lord. Let us speak up and share the treasure we have found. How could we not? "How beautiful on the mountains are the feet of those who bring good news… who proclaim salvation" (Isaiah 52:7).

Loving others well – having the mindset of Christ

"Love is patient, love is kind. It does not envy, it does not boast, it is not proud. It does not dishonor others, it is not self-seeking, it is not easily angered, it keeps no record of wrongs. Love does not delight in evil but rejoices with the truth. It always protects, always trusts, always hopes, always perseveres. Love never fails." (I Corinthians 13:4-8)

"Love one another. As I have loved you, so you must love one another." (John 13:34)

Jesus showed us what perfect love looks like. He taught it and lived it. He is our example. If we want to love like he loved—if we want to love our spouse, our family, our friends and others well—we will follow Jesus' lead.

There is a very specific mindset at the core of the way Jesus lived and loved. It is one that is not popular in our world. It is also counter to what comes naturally to us. But it is the path to loving like Jesus loved. What is it? We will look at several descriptions in the following scriptures. But if I were to sum them up in one word, that word would be *selflessness*.

Let's listen in as the Apostle Paul describes Jesus' mindset toward others:

> Do nothing out of selfish ambition or vain conceit. Rather, in humility value others above yourselves, not looking to your own interests but each of you to the interests of others. In your relationships with one another, have the same mindset as Christ Jesus: Who, being in very nature God, did not consider equality with God something to be used to his own advantage; rather, he made himself nothing by taking the very nature of a servant (Philippians 2:3-7).

Now, let's see what Jesus said about those who want to be his disciples: "Whoever wants to be my disciple must deny themselves and take up their cross daily and follow me" (Luke 9:23).

There are several key elements within these passages from Philippians and Luke. If we want to love like Jesus loved, we are instructed to not be selfish or vain; to not use our position for our own advantage; to look to the interests of others; to value others above ourselves; to take on the nature of a servant; to deny ourselves; and to be humble.

Before looking at how this applies to us, there is a message we should *not* take away from these verses. They are not telling us that

164

some people are worth more than others. Pastor Rick Warren says, "True humility is not thinking less of yourself; it is thinking of yourself less."[4] Every human being is of equal worth. In fact, in these verses we read that Jesus is equal with God (the Father). These scriptures also tell us that Jesus did not use his equality with the Father to his own advantage. Instead, he looked "to the interests of others" by willingly taking on "the very nature of a servant."

In essence, although Jesus was equal with the Father, he willingly set aside his position, humbling himself to serve others. He made the highest good of others his primary consideration, even though it cost him. That is what perfect love looks like.

What would it look like for us to love others selflessly? Considering the feelings and wishes of others; caring for the needs of others at our expense; setting aside our hurt feelings to pray for those who hurt us; and going out of our way to do something nice for others. These are just a few examples. When we live in Christ, he will guide us into what loving well looks like in practical ways.

In summary, loving well is generosity in all of its forms, expressing God's selfless love to others.

Loving others well – an illustration

Jesus gave us this illustration which is recorded in Luke 10:25-37.

The Parable of the Good Samaritan

On one occasion an expert in the law stood up to test Jesus. "Teacher," he asked, "what must I do to inherit eternal life?"

"What is written in the Law?" he replied. "How do you read it?"

He answered, "Love the Lord your God with all your heart and with all your soul and with all your strength and with all your mind"; and, "Love your neighbor as yourself."

"You have answered correctly," Jesus replied. "Do this and you will live." But he wanted to justify himself, so he asked Jesus, "And who is my neighbor?"

In reply Jesus said: "A man was going down from Jerusalem to Jericho, when he was attacked by robbers. They stripped him of his clothes, beat him and went away, leaving him half dead. A priest happened to be going down the same road, and when he saw the man, he passed by on the other side. So too, a Levite, when he came to the place and saw him, passed by on the other side. But a Samaritan, as he traveled, came where the man was; and when he saw him, he took pity on him. He went to him and bandaged his wounds, pouring on oil and wine. Then he put the man on his own donkey, brought him to an inn and took care of him. The next day he took out two denarii and gave them to the innkeeper. "Look after him," he said, "and when I return, I will reimburse you for any extra expense you may have."

"Which of these three do you think was a neighbor to the man who fell into the hands of the robbers?"

The expert in the law replied, "The one who had mercy on him."

Jesus told him, "Go and do likewise."

In response to this parable, Dr. Martin Luther King, Jr. had this to say: "I imagine that the first question the priest and the Levite asked was: 'If I stop to help this man, what will happen to me?' But by the very nature of his concern, the good Samaritan reversed the question: 'If I do not stop to help this man, what will happen to him?'[5] This is certainly what our Lord said when he looked at our world and chose to come to us. He intentionally and willingly put us first. This is what fulfilling relationships are made of. *This* is how we love well.

Many people in our world have needs—from our closest family and friends to those in our community, and across the globe. God wants to love and care for others through us. His love in our hearts compels us to be that good Samaritan.

In the process of loving others in practical ways, may we always keep sight of the fact that the greatest need we all have is our need for Christ and the "life that is truly life," which is only found in him. There is no better way to express love for someone than to share the gospel with them.

God wants to transform us, our marriages, our families, our communities, and beyond. Let us never underestimate the power of his love lived out through our lives and in our world.

"May our Lord Jesus Christ himself and God our Father, who loved us and by his grace gave us eternal encouragement and good hope, encourage your hearts and strengthen you in every good deed and word" (2 Thessalonians 2:16-17).

OUR ETERNAL HOME

Jesus said, "'I am the resurrection and the life. The one who believes in me will live, even though they die." (John 11:25)

"Because I live, you also will live.' " (John 14:19)

At our journey's end, God will welcome his children home. We read in 2 Corinthians 4:14, "we know that the one who raised the Lord Jesus from the dead will also raise us with Jesus."

There are many details we don't know about our life to come, likely because it is something we cannot yet fully understand… "What no eye has seen, what no ear has heard, and what no human mind has conceived'—the things God has prepared for those who love him." (I Corinthians 2:9). Whatever our eternal home is like, I'm sure it will be amazing because we will be in the presence of the One we love—the One who loves us with a perfect love.

"Therefore, as you received Christ Jesus the Lord, so walk in him, rooted and built up in him and established in the faith, just as you were taught."
(Colossians 2:6-7 ESV)

Closing

"Seek the Lord while He may be found" (Isaiah 55:6)

"You can't go back and change the beginning, but you can start where you are and change the ending." (Author unknown)

I have memories of conversations between my grandmother and her sister when they were in their 60s and 70s discussing how amazed they were about how quickly the years flew by. Some of their comments were reflective, and others were quite humorous as they talked about the effects of aging. They've been gone for many years, and now I'm the one in my 60s commenting about how quickly the years pass. In time, my daughter and son-in-law will be doing the same. And on and on it goes.

God created us, and he loves us. He wants us to love him back with our whole heart. He wants us to enjoy life with him now and eternally… life that is truly life. He has allowed us to be here on this earth for just a short while. The choices we make not only impact our lives here and now, but they also determine our eternity.

One day, we will take our final breath, but our soul will live on. There is no better way to live and no better way to die than in Christ. May it be that at the end of our earthly time we will be able to proclaim what the Psalmist wrote: "My flesh and my heart may fail, but God is the strength of my heart and my portion forever." (Psalm 73:26)

"Now to him who is able to do immeasurably more than all we ask or imagine, according to his power that is at work within us, to him be glory in the church and in Christ Jesus throughout all generations, for ever and ever! Amen." (Ephesians 3:20-21)

APPENDIX 1

YOUR NEW LIFE IN CHRIST

Welcome to the family of God!

The day you become a follower of Jesus is a day you will remember for the rest of your life. People experience this life-changing event in different ways. It may evoke in you feelings of relief, joy, or freedom, or you may not feel any emotions at all—just the calm awareness that you have turned a corner in your life and are now embarking on a new path. Whatever your response, you can trust the truth of God's Word, that by sincerely believing, repenting, and professing Christ as Lord of your life, you are now part of his family. Your new life in Christ has begun!

You may have a lot of questions on your mind at this point about prayer, the Bible, church, etc. These and other topics are addressed in Chapter 8 ("Walking with God") so you'll want to read that chapter. There are other questions that apply primarily to new Christians, such as:

"Which translation of the Bible should I use?"

Some people find it helpful to begin with the New Living Translation. Later, when delving into deeper study of the Bible, the New International Version (NIV) and the English Standard Version (ESV) are translations many people use. You can check out these and other translations of the Bible at biblehub.com and biblegateway.com.

"What should I look for in a church?"

A church that teaches the Bible and observes the two ordinances that Jesus established

These are the most important aspects to look for in a church.

Jesus established two ordinances: baptism and communion.

Jesus, who is our example, was baptized (Matthew 3:13-16), and he wants us to be baptized (Matthew 28:19). You will want to be baptized as soon as you can arrange it. Baptism is an outward expression of what has already taken place inwardly. It is declaring your commitment to God and your willingness to obey him. It also acknowledges to your family, friends and others, the importance of the commitment you have made.

Jesus also celebrated communion with his disciples and said we should do this in remembrance of him. Churches observe communion weekly, monthly or on other set schedules.

A church that offers opportunities for you to grow in understanding the Bible and to mature in Christ

Bible study groups are a great way to learn God's Word. Some churches also offer classes for in-depth teaching on specific topics.

A church where love for God and others is expressed

How do the people in the church interact with each other? Does the church promote sharing the gospel? How does the church minister to the hurting and those in need? What outreach does the church do in the community and beyond?

You will probably want to visit several churches before you decide. Pray for God to guide you in this process.

Have realistic expectations. When I first became a Christian, I thought I would find the perfect church. My expectations were unrealistic. Let me share with you what I came to realize:

No church is perfect—because the church is actually the people, not the building. Any group setting we find ourselves in, including church, will include people who are just like us: imperfect. Nevertheless, many wonderful churches exist with people who are walking with the Lord, worshipping together, learning together, and serving together—and they would be happy to have you join them!

Once again, congratulations on your new life in Christ!
May God bless you as you seek to know him and love him
with your whole heart.

SHARE THE GOOD NEWS ... Share *A Heart for God!*

A Heart for God was written to share the gospel message—from reasons to believe it, to what it means to become a follower of Christ and to walk with him on our life's journey.

Share *A Heart for God* eBook

A Heart for God is available as a free eBook at <u>heartforgod.org</u>—and not just for a limited time. It will always be free on this website. Share this link with others.

Share a printed copy of *A Heart for God*

For details on how you can purchase (or print) *A Heart for God*, go to www.heartforgod.org. *One hundred percent of all royalties received from the sale of A Heart for God are used to further promote this book.*

NOTES

INTRODUCTION

1. James Sire, "8 Questions Every Worldview Must Answer," www.christianity.com 2014

SECTION ONE—REASONS TO BELIEVE - INTRODUCTION

1. Josh McDowell, "From Skepticism to Belief: A Conversation with Josh McDowell" by Jim Dailey, Decision Magazine 2005

2. Lexico.com

3. 1 Peter 3:15 ESV

4. C. S. Lewis, *God in the Dock* (Harper Collins Publishers, 1970) page 43 (electronic version)

CHAPTER ONE—PURSUING TRUTH

1. Charles Colson, *The Good Life* (Tyndale House Publishers, 2005) page 10 (electronic version)

2. Definitions.net

3. "Galaxies Galore! Hubble's Last 'Frontier Fields' Image Live Shots," www.svs.gsfc.nasa.gov/12596

4. History.com editors, www.history.com/topics/inventions/isaac-newton

5. Lexico.com

6. Oxford Dictionaries Word of the Year, www.languages.oup.com/word-of-the-year/2016

7. Lexico.com

8. Pbs.org, glossary

9. Vince Vitale, *Jesus Among Secular Gods*, co-authored by Ravi Zacharias (Faith Words, Hachette Book Group)

10. John Lennox, video posted on YouTube by IDquest, "God and Stephen Hawking – John Lennox, PhD", 2013

CHAPTER TWO—REASONS TO BELIEVE IN GOD

1. C. S. Lewis, as quoted by Stoyan Zaimov, "Christian Apologist: 10 Reasons for the Fall of Atheism", The Christian Post, 2013

2. Ray Comfort, *The Evidence Bible* (Bridge-Logos Foundation, 2011)

3. Video posted on YouTube by tubester4567, "Richard Dawkins vs. Cardinal George Pell on Q & A", 2012

4. Ibid.

5. Francis Crick, as quoted by New York Times, *"Is There Life Elsewhere, and Did it Come Here?"* 1981

6. Norman L. Geisler and Frank Turek, *I Don't Have Enough Faith to be an Atheist* (Illinois, Crossway, Good News Publishers, 2004)

7. Neil deGrasse Tyson, *Astrophysics for People in a Hurry* (New York, W. W. Norton & Company, 2017), p. 17

8. Wikipedia.com/Robert Jastrow

9. Robert Jastrow, as quoted by Bill Durbin in the article, "A Scientist Caught Between Two Faiths", www.christianitytoday.com, 1982

10. Robert Jastrow, *God and the Astronomers* (New York, Warner Books, Inc., 1978), pp. 3–4

11. Paul Davies, *The Cosmic Blueprint: New Discoveries in Nature's Creative Ability to Order the Universe* (Simon & Schuster, 1988), page 203

12. John O'Keefe, *Show Me God* (Searchlight Publications, 1995), page 200

13. NASA, asd.gsfc.nasa.gov/blueshift/index.php/2015/07/22

14. Genome.gov/about-genomics/fact-sheet/A-Brief-Guide-to-Genomics

15. Stephen C. Meyer, interview with Biola Magazine, "Can DNA prove the existence of an intelligent designer?", 2010

16. Genome.gov/human-genome-project

17. Antony Flew, *There is a God: How the World's Most Notorious Atheist Changed His Mind*, 2007 (New York, Harper Collins Publishers, 2008)

18. Judith Ball, personal correspondence

19. Stephen C. Meyer, interview with Biola Magazine, "Can DNA prove the existence of an intelligent designer?", 2010

20. Francis S. Collins, article by cnn.com, "Collins: Why this scientist believes in God"

21. Ibid.

22. Francis S. Collins, vimeo.com/162771029, Alpha Film Series: "Is There More to Life than This?", approximately the 10 minute mark

23. Ibid.

24. Wikipedia.com, Georges Lemaitre

25. Joseph H. Taylor, Jr., as quoted by Tihomir Dimitrov, nobelists.net, in article, "Nobel Laureate Joseph H. Taylor, Jr.: Scientific Discovery Is also a Religious Discovery", www.2012daily.com

26. Louis Pasteur, as quoted by Scott Youngren in "Quotes about God to consider … if you think science leads to atheism", www.goodevidence.com, 2010

27. Arthur L. Schawlow, as quoted by Scott Youngren in "Quotes about God to consider … if you think science leads to atheism", www.goodevidence.com, 2010

28. Elaine Howard Ecklund, as quoted by David Ruth in article, "Misconceptions of science and religion found in new study", 2014

29. C. S. Lewis, as quoted by cslewisinstitute.org in article, "Christianity Makes Sense of the World", 2013

30. John Lennox, God's Undertaker: Has Science Buried God?, (Lion Hudson, 2007), p. 174

CHAPTER THREE—REASONS TO BELIEVE THE BIBLE IS RELIABLE

1. Charles W. Colson, Loving God (Michigan, Zondervan, 1987), p. 55

2. Wycliffe.net/statistics, October 201

3. Biblica.com/resources/bible-faqs/is-the-bible-inspired

4. Ibid.

5. Ibid.

6. Ibid.

7. Daniel B. Wallace, as quoted in interview with Justin Taylor, www.thegospelcoalition.org, "An Interview with Daniel B. Wallace on the New Testament Manuscripts" 2012

8. Peter Gurry, "The Number of Variants in the Greek New Testament: A Proposed Estimate" , Cambridge University Press, 2016, p. 12

9. Daniel B. Wallace, as quoted by Gary D. Myers in article by New Orleans Baptist Theological Seminary's Vision Magazine, "Greer-Heard '08 focuses on New Testament reliability"

10. Daniel B. Wallace, as interviewed by Justin Taylor of The Gospel Coalition, posted on March 12, 2012 ("An Interview with Daniel B. Wallace on the New Testament Manuscripts"). Much of this information is also found in more detail in Wallace's book, *Reinventing Jesus – What the DaVinci Code and Other Novel Speculations Don't Tell You*, co-authored with J. Ed Komoszewski and M. James Sawyer (Michigan, Kregel Publications, 2006)

11. Ibid.

12. Ibid.

13. Ibid., and quote "to some degree" on page 60 of book

14. Daniel B. Wallace, as quoted in interview with Justin Taylor, www.thegospelcoalition.org, "An Interview with Daniel B. Wallace on the New Testament Manuscripts" 2012

15. Norman Geisler, article by Southeast Evangelical Seminary, "Has the Bible Been Accurately Copied Down Through the Centuries?"

16. Bart Ehrman, Misquoting Jesus (New York, Harper San Francisco, 2005), pp. 252-253. This book has been released in several versions. Not all versions contain the Q & A section at the back of the book with Ehrman, which is the source of this quote.

17. Robert B. Stewart, through personal correspondence

18. David Murray, article on www.christianity.com, "The Biggest 'Contradiction' in the Bible", 2014

19. Biblestudytools.com/lexicons/hebrew

20. Biblestudytools.com/lexicons/greek

21. J. Warner Wallace, article on www.coldcasechristianity.com, "Verifiability is a Christian Distinctive", 2015. Used by permission.

22. Sheri Bell, article on www.josh.org, "Archaeology Helps to Confirm the Historicity of the Bible", 2018

23. John Stonestreet, in article co-authored with Roberto Rivera on www.breakpoint.org, "The Reliability of Scripture", 2017

24. J. Warner Wallace, article on www.coldcasechristianity.com, "A Brief Sample of Old Testament Archaeological Corroboration", 2018. Used by permission.

25. Dewayne Bryant, in article on www.apologeticspress.com, "Canaanite DNA and the Biblical Canon", 2017

26. Article on www.josh.org, "Does Archaeological Evidence Prove the Bible? Do Archeological Discoveries Relate to Events in Scripture?"

CHAPTER FOUR—REASONS TO BELIEVE THE CLAIMS OF JESUS

1. James Allen Francis, as quoted on www.bartleby.com

2. J. Warner Wallace, article on www.coldcasechristianity.com, "Who is Jesus According to Other Religions?", 2017. Used by permission.

3. J. Warner Wallace, article on www.coldcasechristianity.com, "Unbelievable? Is There Enough Evidence Beyond the Gospels to Make their Testimony Reliable?", 2017. Used by permission.

4. Simon Gathercole, article on www.theguardian.com, "What is the Historical Evidence that Jesus Christ Lived and Died?", 2017

5. Literarydevices.com

6. Sheri Bell, article on www.josh.org, "Only One Person Has Fulfilled All Old Testament Messianis Prophesy. Jesus!"

7. Josh McDowell and Sean McDowell, PhD, *Evidence that Demands a Verdict*, (Tennessee, Thomas Nelson, 2017), page 46

8. C. S. Lewis, *The Essential C. S. Lewis* (Touchstone, 1996), pages 331-332

9. J. Warner Wallace, article on www.coldcasechristianity.com, "Is Jesus Simply a Retelling of the Horus Mythology?". Used by permission.

10. Ibid.

11. Josh McDowell and Sean McDowell, PhD, *Evidence that Demands a Verdict*, (Tennessee, Thomas Nelson, 2017), page 311

12. Paul Rhodes Eddy and Gregory A. Boyd, The Jesus Legend: A Case for the Historical Reliability of the Synoptic Gospels (Michigan, Baker Publishing Group, 2007), pages 139-140

13. Kenneth Boa, article, "How Accurate is the Bible?" on www.cslewisinstitute.org. Winter 2009 issue of Knowing and Doing.

14. Sean McDowell, article on seanmcdowell.org, "The Biggest Issue that Caused Me to Doubt My Faith", 2018

15. Ibid.

16. Time.com article by Heba Hasan, "Author 'Predicts' Titanic Sinking 14 Years Earlier" 2012

17. C. S. Lewis, Mere Christianity (New York, McMillan Publishing, 1952) pages 55-56

18. Mark Strauss, in article on www.zondervanacademic.com, "4 ways the Gospels disagree and why you can still trust the Bible", 2017. Used by permission.

19. Ibid.

20. Ibid.

21. Michael R. Licona, in interview with Jonathan Petersen, "Why Are There Differences in the Gospels?: An Interview with Michael R. Licona", 2017

22. Ibid.

23. Ibid.

24. William Lane Craig, as interviewed by Lee Stroebel for the book, *The Case for Easter* (Michigan, Zondervan, 1998) page 45

25. Oxforddictionary.com

26. Gary Habermas, article, "The Minimal Facts Approach to the Resurrection of Jesus: The Role of Methodology as a Crucial Component in Establishing Historicity (Liberty University), 2012

27. Gary Habermas, article, "Surprising Scholarly Agreement on Facts That Support Jesus' Resurrection" 2016

28. Ibid.

29. Lucian of Samosata, from The Passing of Peregrinus, as reported by Reformed Wiki, posted 2020

30. Flavius Josephus, as quoted on Wikipedia

31. William D. Edwards, Wesley J. Gabel, Floyd Hosmer as reported in the article, "On the Physical Death of Jesus Christ" in the Journal of the American Medical Association, 1986

32. Peter Kreeft and Ronald K. Tacelli article, "Rejecting the Swoon Theory: 9 Reasons Why Jesus Did Not Faint on the Cross," excerpted from *Handbook of Catholic Apologists* (Ignatius Press, 1994)

33. Matt Perman, article on www.desiringgod.org, "Historical Evidence for the Resurrection", 2007

34. Ibid.

35. J. Warner Wallace, article on www.coldcasechristianity.com, "The Evidentially Diverse Resurrection Appearances of Jesus," 2014

36. Ibid.

37. Peter Kreeft, on www.peterkreeft.com, "Evidence for the Resurrection of Christ"

38. Sean McDowell, from video on YouTube, "Did the Apostles Die as Martyrs?", posted February 22, 2016

39. Gary Habermas and Michael Licona, The Case for the Resurrection of Jesus (Michigan, Kregel Publications, 2004)

40. Wikipedia, "Tacitus on Christ"

41. Sean McDowell, from video on YouTube, "Did the Apostles Die as Martyrs?", posted February 22, 2016

42. James Allen Francis, as quoted on www.bartleby.com

SECTION TWO—ENCOUNTERING GOD—INTRODUCTION

1. Jon Morrison, *Clear Minds & Dirty Feet: A Reason to Hope, a Message to Share* (Canada, Apologetics Canada Publishing, 2013)

CHAPTER FIVE—WHAT GOD IS LIKE

1. J. I. Packer, *Evangelism and the Sovereignty of God* (InterVarsity Press, 2012) chapter 2, page 9 (electronic version)

2. Norman L. Geisler and Frank Turek, I Don't Have Enough Faith to Be an Atheist (Illinois, Crossway, 2004), page 352

3. Ibid.

4. Luke Wayne, article on Christian Apologetics & Research Ministry (www.carm.org), "Is God personal?" 2017

5. Ibid.

6. J. Hampton Keathley, III, article on www.bible.org, "What God is Like", 2004

7. Article on www.gotquestions.org, "What does it mean that God is light?"

8. Lexico.com

9. J. Hampton Keathley, III, article on www.bible.org, "What God is Like", 2004

10. Article on www.allaboutgod.com,, "God is Just", 2002

11. Article on www.gotquestions.org, "What is the grace of God?"

12. Arthur W. Pink, as quoted in The Wisdom of Arthur W. Pink (Simon & Schuster, 2013), page 430

CHAPTER SIX—GOD'S RELATIONSHIP WITH MANKIND

1. Jeff Cavins, article on www.media.ascensionpress.com, "You Were Made for Narrative, But Do You Know Which One?", 2020

2. Francis Crick, The Astonishing Hypothesis (New York, Touchstone, 1995)

3. Richard Dawkins, River Out of Eden (New York, Basic Books, 1995), page 133

4. Natasha Crain, article on www.christianmomthoughts.com, "5 Ways Christians are Getting Swept into a Secular Worldview in this Cultural Moment", 2020

5. Francis S. Collins, article by cnn.com, "Collins: Why this scientist believes in God". See full quote on page 41 of this book.

6. John Frady, personal correspondence

7. Author unknown

8. Jerry Bridges, Trusting God: Even When Life Hurts (NavPress, 2008)

9. Rick Warren, booklet: "What on Earth Am I Here For?", page 20

10. C. S. Lewis, The Problem of Pain

11. Abdu Murray, ,*Grand Central Question* (Illinois, Inter Varsity Press, 2014), page 109

12. J. Warner Wallace, article on www.coldcasechristianity.com. Used by permission.

13. C. S. Lewis, *Mere Christianity*, (Harper Collins, 1952-1996) page 48

14. Max Lucado, article on www.foxnews.com, "Max Lucado: Texas high school shooting – This evil will not last forever", 2018

CHAPTER SEVEN—YOU ARE INVITED

1. Strong's Concordance, biblestudytools.com/concordances/strongs-exhaustive-concordance

CHAPTER EIGHT—WALKING WITH GOD

1. Dictionary.com

2. Article on www.gotquestions.org, "I am a new Christian. What is the next step?"

3. Rick Warren, an article on pastorrick.com, "God Says Respond to Unfairness with Love" 9/16/20

4. Rick Warren, *The Purpose Driven Life* (Zondervan, 2012)

5. Martin Luther King, Jr., *Strength to Love* (Minnesota, Fortress Press, 2010) page 26

ABOUT THE AUTHOR

Vicki Lynn Gordy is passionate about sharing with others what she discovered many years ago—why the claims of Christianity are believable and worth embracing. She lives in the New Orleans area which is also home to the loves of her life—her daughter, son-in-law, and granddaughter. Vicki works for a faith-based agency helping those impacted by domestic violence. For helpful information on a variety of topics, check out Vicki's website, vickigordy.com.